Teenagers

Resource Books for Teachers
series editor Alan Maley

Teenagers

Gordon Lewis

OXFORD
UNIVERSITY PRESS

OXFORD
UNIVERSITY PRESS

Great Clarendon Street, Oxford OX2 6DP

Oxford University Press is a department of the University of Oxford.
It furthers the University's objective of excellence in research, scholarship,
and education by publishing worldwide in

Oxford New York

Auckland Cape Town Dar es Salaam Hong Kong Karachi
Kuala Lumpur Madrid Melbourne Mexico City Nairobi
New Delhi Shanghai Taipei Toronto

With offices in

Argentina Austria Brazil Chile Czech Republic France Greece
Guatemala Hungary Italy Japan Poland Portugal Singapore
South Korea Switzerland Thailand Turkey Ukraine Vietnam

OXFORD and OXFORD ENGLISH are registered trade marks of
Oxford University Press in the UK and in certain other countries

ISBN-13: 987 019 442577 3

Printed in China

Acknowledgments

> When I was a boy of fourteen, my father was so ignorant I could hardly stand to have the old man around. But when I got to be twenty-one, I was astonished at how much he had learned in seven years.
> Mark Twain, 'Old Times on the Mississippi', *Atlantic Monthly*, 1874.

I'd like to thank my family, Katja, Kira, and Nicholas for putting up with an absent husband/father as I worked to get this manuscript right. I'd also like to thank Bruce and Julia at OUP for their insightful comments and suggestions.

Finally, an extra special thanks to Guenther Bedson for supplying some great ideas and being a good friend even in difficult times.

The author and publisher are grateful to those who have given permission to reproduce the following extracts and adaptations of copyright material:

'How to read stock tables' chart from the New York Stock Exchange website at http://www.nyse.com/pdfs/NYSE_posterA_Mech.pdf. Reproduced by kind permission of NYSE.

Illustrations by Stefan Chabluc, p. 63; Ann Johns pp. 67, 76, and 102.

Photographs courtesy of:
Corbis, p. 18 British Museum/photo Bettmann Archive; p. 95 Taj Mahal/photo Will & Deni McIntyre, Crazy Horse Memorial by Korczak Ziolkowski/photo Nik Wheeler © Crazy Horse Foundation, Lincoln Memorial by Daniel Chester French/photo Craig Lovell, Vietnam Veterans Memorial/photo Bettmann Archive.
Alamy, p. 57 (tiles/Richard Heyes, milk/Cephas Picture Library).
Cover photography courtesy Getty Images/Jon Riley.

Contents

2 Creative and critical thinking tasks

3 Teenager topics

The author and series editor

Gordon Lewis earned a BSc in Languages and Linguistics from Georgetown University, Washington DC, and an MSc from the Monterey Institute of International Studies, Monterey, California. In 1991 he founded the Children's Language School in Berlin, Germany, which was sold to Berlitz in 1999. From 1999 to 2001 he was Director of Berlitz Kids Germany and developed similar programs for Berlitz across Europe. From 2001 to 2003 he was Director of Instructor Training and Development for Berlitz Kids in Princeton, New Jersey. He is currently Director of Product Development for Kaplan English Programs in New York City, and is also on the committee of the IATEFL Young Learners Special Interest Group where he works as co-coordinator for events. He is author of *Games for Children* and *The Internet and Young Learners*, both in the *Resource Books for Teachers* series published by Oxford University Press.

Alan Maley worked for The British Council from 1962 to 1988, serving as English Language Officer in Yugoslavia, Ghana, Italy, France, and China, and as Regional Representative in South India (Madras). From 1988 to 1993 he was Director-General of the Bell Educational Trust, Cambridge. From 1993 to 1998 he was Senior Fellow in the Department of English Language and Literature of the National University of Singapore, and from 1998 to 2002 he was Director of the graduate programme at Assumption University, Bangkok. He is currently a freelance consultant. Among his publications are *Literature*, in this series, *Beyond Words*, *Sounds Interesting*, *Sounds Intriguing*, *Words*, *Variations on a Theme*, and *Drama Techniques in Language Learning* (all with Alan Duff), *The Mind's Eye* (with Françoise Grellet and Alan Duff), *Learning to Listen* and *Poem into Poem* (with Sandra Moulding), *Short and Sweet*, and *The English Teacher's Voice*.

Foreword

Until now, all the books in the Oxford Resource Books for Teachers series have addressed two main types of learner: 'adults, especially young adults' and 'Young Learners'. It is clear however, that a large proportion of all learners of English as a second or foreign language is made up of 'teenagers', a group with special characteristics which falls somewhere between these two groups. While it is true that many of the activities in titles for the two main groups are also suitable, with or without adaptation, for teenagers, this book is the first to address the specific needs of the teenage group explicitly and directly. As such, it is worthy of special attention.

It is common to regard learners in the teenage bracket (12–19 years old: though this book concentrates on those aged 12–17) as 'a problem'. They are going through profound physical changes, accompanied by an often anxious period of self-awareness and self-examination, as well as a sudden growth of critical perceptions about the world they inhabit. They are frequently labelled as difficult, moody, restless, intransigent, undisciplined …, and a host of other negative attributes. Yet, as some second language acquisition research shows, they are also at an ideal age to learn things, including languages. It is the author's contention that, if we regard teenagers as a golden opportunity rather than as a noxious problem, then we can tap into the abundant energy, curiosity, and critical awareness which this age group displays.

The author emphasizes that one of the keys to accessing this energy and to enlisting the co-operation of teenagers is respect and tolerance for them. Teachers need to demonstrate that they can empathize with the concerns and preoccupations of these learners, but without condescension and without themselves trying to 'be' teenagers.

The activities themselves go well beyond the usual superficial topics of teen culture, such as pop music, fashion, drugs, sport, etc., and seek to engage the learners in matters of deeper concern, such as self-esteem, peer pressure, relationships, identity, ethical concerns, and critical thinking. The author presents a set of motivating, uncomplicated activities, and contrives to give a novel twist even to those which may at first sight be familiar to teachers.

It is the quality of the teacher–student relationship which holds the key to success with teaching teenagers. This book will be a major contribution to building relationships based on trust and mutual respect.

Alan Maley

Introduction

Teenagers—the word often puts fear in the heart of the language teacher. Visions of bored students slouched in their chairs, or class clowns playing practical jokes, can sap the confidence of the most experienced teachers. In the world of ELT, there can surely be no other age group with as bad an image as teenagers.

Do they deserve this reputation? Is it really fair to see teenagers this way? This negative view towards teenagers blinds us to the exciting sides of this age group. The things that can make teenagers difficult are often the very same attributes that can make working with them so enriching. It is a question of perspective—and a teacher's attitude towards the teenager will have a huge influence on the quality of their interaction. Try and think back to when you were a teenager. Can you remember a teacher or person who made a lasting impression and motivated you? What characteristics did he or she have?

One thing that I have heard from teenagers again and again is that they want to be treated with respect. To be condescending or 'teach down' to them is a recipe for disaster. This does not mean you should 'play teenager' yourself. You are not a teenager! You are still a power figure, representing authority, and you need to keep that distinction clear if you want to maintain a good relationship with your students.

Remember, teenagers have their own culture. This culture has its own icons and even a distinct language. In order to appeal to teenagers, many teachers feel they have to become teenagers themselves. They try really hard to be 'cool'. Teenagers rarely respect this kind of behavior. They want the teacher to respect their culture, not co-opt it. There is nothing wrong with letting the students know you are familiar with some fads and trends, but do not try to dress, talk, or act like them, unless you enjoy being ridiculed.

Teenagers can be quite emotional. Everything is so momentous and all-consuming. When teachers claim that teenagers are lethargic and hard to motivate, I am always surprised. I have never known a student of this age NOT to have had an opinion on a matter, provided the subject was of direct relevance to their lives. If you can set up activities which challenge teenagers to think, you are assured of getting lots of impassioned input.

Simply introducing English through popular teen culture will not sustain motivation. To be successful with teenagers, we need to dig deeper and find the themes which transcend generations. Whether you were born in 1950, 1970, or 1990, issues such as:

- self-esteem
- peer pressure
- ethics
- finding one's own identity
- dealing with relationships

to name but a few, will all have relevance to your life in one way or another. If the teacher can design activities which integrate these types of elemental issues, the students themselves will bring the input to relate it back to their current reality.

Of course not every activity in a resource book can be full of such deeply personal significance. On a broader scale, we need to:

- engage teenagers by creating language awareness activities which foster an understanding of, and an interest in, how languages function.
- encourage students to become precise critical thinkers and to link their language study to other areas of their education.
- promote group work and collaborative learning through class projects.

Finally, recent studies have suggested that the teenage years may be the time when students learn languages fastest and most efficiently. Childlike playfulness and an adult-like ability to hypothesize and think critically combine to establish a balance between acquisition and learning which is not always available to learners at other ages.

What is a teenager?

Before we move forward, let's define what a teenager is. A teenager is a young person between the ages of approximately twelve and nineteen. Most experts split this age range into three distinct groups:

- young teenagers, aged 12–14
- middle teenagers, aged 14–17
- late teenagers, aged 17–19

In this book we will focus on young and middle teenagers—students attending middle and high school. In my experience, late teenagers are in most ways young adults. Many have jobs and live on their own. Some are even married. In short, they are in the real world and have full responsibility over their own destiny. Young and middle teenagers, on the other hand, are still finding themselves. They have tasted independence but are not fully ready to fly.

Features of adolescence

Young teenagers (12–14 years old)

Young teenagers are undergoing such dramatic changes in every aspect of their lives that it should be little wonder that they can be a bit moody and difficult to handle at times. To understand young teenagers, it is important to know that the most important thing in their lives at this point is *themselves*. This natural egocentrism is paired with lots of emotion. Young teenagers will feel that nobody understands them because they feel nobody has ever felt the way they do. This can lead to quite a bit of melodrama—a characteristic which can be very useful in a language classroom if it is organized in an unthreatening way.

Physical changes

The most obvious change young teenagers are going through is physical. Most of us can remember the small thirteen-year-old boy or shy awkward girl whom we could not even recognize two years later. Each child goes through these changes at a different speed, with girls maturing much faster and towering over their male classmates at this age. These sudden and dramatic changes make teenagers very sensitive to their appearance. Their position in school society and hence their level of self-esteem and self-confidence are closely tied to how they look.

Social changes

Young teenagers definitely want to belong to the 'pack'. Groups are very important as a means of establishing identity and gaining confidence. Friendships and peer groups begin to influence students strongly, as they assert their independence by moving away from parents and finding new role models. Young teenagers find comfort and identity in youth culture as reflected in fads and cliques. Of course, not all students readily 'fit in', especially if they are new to a school or socially or physically awkward. These students can feel isolated and lonely. They are also subject to bullying and even to physical abuse. Be aware of such situations in your classroom and seek help from a counsellor if you see serious problems developing.

While young teenagers have certainly discovered the opposite sex, the girl–boy divide is still pronounced. Young teenagers will still tend to have same-sex friends and move in same-sex groups.

Young teenagers find themselves with increased responsibility for their lives. Parents and other adults begin talking to them on a more even level. Young teenagers now need to make decisions and develop a degree of independence. This newly-found independence often comes with new privileges. These new privileges often whet the young teen's appetite for more, creating potential conflict between parents and teachers. Young teenagers waver between independence and a need for security. They have one foot in the adult world and one in the world of their childhood.

As a teacher, you walk a fine line with this age group. You must give them responsibility, or else they may be offended and withdraw. However, it would be equally problematic to treat teenagers as adults. They still need guidance.

Thinking skills

Young teenagers have a longer concentration span than primary-age children. They can focus on a single project for an entire lesson and do not need a constant change of activity as younger students do.

Being more independent, young teenagers readily engage in group work. However, this needs to be monitored closely as young teenagers often 'regress' into more childlike behavior and fool around. Often this is part of showing off to their peers.

One of the most marked changes in the transition from childhood to adolescence is the young teen's ability to think abstractly. While still rooted very much in the here and now, young teenagers begin to understand that the world is complex and they strive to create a 'system' to analyze what they see. They are developing a world view independent from their parents. Young teenagers test hypotheses and think critically about abstract ideas and concepts. But since they are relatively inexperienced, they tend to paint their reality in very broad strokes.

New to the complexity of the world, young teenagers have a tendency to think they have 'figured things out'. In the young teen mind there is little room for grey areas. It's a black and white world. Opinions are very strong, especially when it comes to 'larger' questions such as morality or politics. Young teenagers often believe what they think and what everyone else thinks is essentially the same. This newly-found ability to hypothesize often results in teenagers seeing theories as facts when it is coupled with their still very concrete worldview.

Middle teenagers (14–17 years old)

Physical changes

By the end of the middle teen years, full physical growth has in most cases been nearly achieved. Physically, boys have caught up with girls. This is not only the case on the outside. Internally, boys and girls of this age have moved through puberty and have matured to become adults.

Social skills

Middle teenagers exhibit strong abilities to work independently. They are good planners and can manage group work with less supervision than younger teenagers. As they develop their own sense of identity and place in society, middle teenagers are less reliant on the group for support. In fact, some older teenagers may even shun groups, creating a problem for some teachers.

Middle teenagers are very aware of the opposite sex. Same-sex groups get replaced by girl–boy relationships. While friends are still very important, group identity loses some of its importance and is replaced by individual relationships.

Thinking skills

Unlike younger teenagers, middle teenagers learn that there is not only ONE answer to every question. They understand that things are relative and that we all have to make difficult choices. This new ability to reason is particularly evident when discussing morals and ethics, and leads to more tolerance than their younger peers, who measure people and behavior in absolute terms. There is also greater potential for confusion, as older teenagers realize that not everything is black and white. With more confidence in their own identity, older teenagers take a more differentiated view of the world. They are more willing to accept that there is more than one solution to a problem.

Classroom management tips

In talks with teenagers, one of the most important points they make is that they want to be treated with respect. To condescend or 'teach down' to teenagers will have a very negative effect on discipline. However, as already stated, it is very important not to 'play teenager' yourself in an effort to ingratiate yourself or appear 'cool'. Let's face it: you are not a teen and never will be one in the eyes of your students. Show an interest in teen culture. Treat teen ideas with respect, but take advantage of the fact that you are the adult to maintain control. Despite teen rebelliousness, you are still the authority figure and you need to make clear that the respect you show to them must be returned back to you in the form of appropriate classroom behavior. In other words, be friendly, but don't expect to be your students' friend.

Puberty is a difficult time for all teenagers, but in certain circumstances students can have serious emotional problems which require attention. In puberty, teenagers are confronted with very adult problems which they may not know how to cope with (such as pregnancy, substance abuse, violence). Some students will have difficulty confiding in parents or classmates when they have such problems and they may turn to you for help and support. In such a situation it is important to know how to react and who to turn to for advice. If you have not been trained in counselling, do not try and deal with a student's problems on your own. This can backfire and lead to very serious consequences for you and the student. Instead, get information and learn where to turn when such a situation arises. In the Appendix there is a list of websites which can provide you with some guidance.

Keeping these fundamental points in mind, here are some classroom management tips that have worked for teachers I know.

Make students responsible for their actions

Teenagers strive to be independent. They want more responsibility. Grant this responsibility and all the rights and obligations it implies, but hold students accountable for both their work and their behavior. Negotiate rules with the students. Let them have input, and then hold them to the decisions that have been made. They will understand this. At the beginning of term, it may be worth drawing up a 'contract' with your students to outline mutual rights and responsibilities that you have agreed.

Encourage students to be honest and candid

Teenagers often say exactly what they think. Encourage them to speak their mind. Afford opportunities for students to express their opinions. However, remember that teenagers can also be disrespectful and sometimes cruel. Establish limits. Do not tolerate disrespect.

Get students involved in setting class goals

Negotiate the syllabus with your students. Allow students to make suggestions about how to conduct activities. Explain your expectations and pre-requisites for the class, and let the students brainstorm possible courses of action. Give the students choices. Have the confidence to relinquish control and the determination to get it back if students take advantage.

Take an interest in your students' lives

Teenagers, especially younger ones are the center of their own attention. Ask questions about the student. How do they feel? What do they think? Treat the teen as a mature thinker, even if the ideas he or she expresses are very dogmatic and one-sided.

Teenagers and technology

Ten years ago it might still have been possible to discuss the teenage experience without reference to technology. Today, technology has an enormous impact on all aspects of teenage life which simply cannot be ignored. The implications for the classroom are huge.

Teenagers today grow up in an information world. They are surrounded by media. This access to information has put teenagers more in control of their lives than previous generations. Today's teenagers are growing up faster than in the past. They are expected to 'make sense' of the information they receive at an earlier age. While many primary school students will have been exposed to computers and will have mastered the technology, it is in their early teenagers that most begin to interact autonomously with the medium and learn its true power.

In the digital world, information is constantly changing. Teaching a subject is not as simple as A, B, C, or point 1, point 2, point 3. Entry points and exit points and the paths between them are increasingly student-determined. Today's teenager is used to exploratory learning. This level of independence needs to be extended to activities in the language-learning classroom. As a teacher of teenagers you must have the confidence to take a step back and encourage autonomous learning. Encourage discovery learning but be specific in establishing expectations and explaining steps in the process.

Today's teenagers feel 'connected' to the rest of the world—and indeed they are. There is definitely a global youth culture—and not one dominated solely by media and commercial interests. Teenagers have always sought avenues of self-expression. Today, email, chat, instant messaging, and especially blogs, provide teenagers with opportunities to speak their mind and share these thoughts with the rest of the world. If the students know that the information on their blog is going online, they will make an effort to get everything right. This supports accuracy and fluency in the language classroom.

The ability to 'self-publish' is a particularly compelling aspect of technology for teenagers. Technology can make a school report look like a professional document. New technology allows students to make small movies or audio files with ease. This ability to engage multiple senses through the computer medium can have a great impact on skills work in your classroom, making it possible to do both specific and integrated skills work in authentic, motivating contexts. This is especially useful if you teach a very large class where opportunities for students to practise are limited.

When deciding whether or not to use technology in your classroom, consider the benefits beyond the basic 'coolness' factor. How long will it take the students to complete the task using conventional versus computer approaches? Does the computer medium reinforce the aims of the lesson? For example, using computer software to create a newspaper template in order to create a school newspaper makes a lot of sense, while asking students to 'decorate' a survey worksheet doesn't really 'teach' them anything new, and may not even require any English at all. If you have time, this may not matter that much, but it is advisable to always look for a specific language link in any computer-based activity. I have not written activities in this book which are dependent on computers or the Internet, but I have made suggestions for computer use where appropriate. For ideas and examples of how to integrate technology into these activities, see the website that accompanies this book at www.oup.com/elt/teacher/rbt and also *The Internet* in this series.

Finally, if you have a technology instructor at your school, combine your efforts and integrate language projects and computer science. If you don't have any colleagues for support and you feel unsure of yourself, rest assured—your students will probably be able to help.

Teaching across the curriculum

Over the past decade there has been growing interest in content-based language instruction in the EFL world. Content-based teaching is a method which integrates subject-area content, such as math, science or history, into the foreign-language classroom. Content-based language instruction is not new. It has been a widely practised teaching method in EAL (English as an Additional Language, also known as ESL) situations for almost two decades. In EAL (ESL) contexts, students with limited English are taught to function in mainstream English-speaking classrooms either in an English-speaking country or in schools with English as the medium of instruction. It is only recently that EFL teachers have begun to recognize the benefits of using subject-area content in their foreign-language classrooms. The difference between the two contexts is subtle yet important. In the EAL (ESL) situation the primary goal is to help students meet the expectations of the subject-area classroom, be it math, history, or science. The focus is *learning content through English*. In EFL, the priority remains language development. In other words *learning English through content*.

In Europe, and increasingly in other parts of the world, content-based language teaching has been identified by the broad umbrella term CLIL (Content Language Integrated Learning). This is a slippery concept, with both strong and weak interpretations. Many experts prefer to speak of a CLIL continuum, which spans a range from topic-based EFL to bilingual and immersion programs. Figure 1 shows a simple diagram of the CLIL continuum.

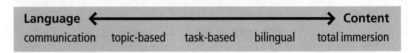

Figure 1

In this book I focus on *learning English through content*. I believe that by using material from the mainstream classroom we can achieve three key objectives:
- We can motivate the students by making English lessons purposeful and immediately relevant.
- We can support their learning and promote thinking skills by working with materials and concepts they are familiar with.
- We can transfer key academic skills from the native language classroom and apply them to language learning, developing what Jim Cummins calls *Cognitive Academic Language Proficiency* (CALP).

Identifying which content to use has always been a difficult issue for proponents of content-based EFL. If you are not a mainstream teacher you may not be familiar with the school curriculum. If you work in a mainstream school, I encourage you to consult with your colleagues and plan lessons together. If you work in a private language school, your task is a bit more difficult. For this reason I have designed many activities as task frameworks, which the students themselves can fill with content.

Remember, where content is concerned in this book, the goal of the activity is not to have the students learn math, science or history, but to learn to talk, or write about these subjects in English. If you are in the enviable position of being able to teach both at the same time, all the better for you!

For more information on CLIL and CBT (Content-Based Teaching) see *Teaching Other Subjects Through English* in this series.

How to use this book

Level

We use five levels in this book. Table 1 on page 14 gives a short description of each level. You will notice that there are not many activities aimed at beginning-level students. This is because it is assumed that most students in middle or high school will have been studying English for at least a year. Likewise, there are not many activities solely for advanced levels, since few teenagers reach that level, but activities suitable for Upper-Intermediate and above can be used with advanced students.

It is important to understand that these levels are merely guidelines. Student levels can vary substantially by skill. Some students may have very strong writing skills but struggle with speaking. Others may have difficulty reading because their native alphabet is different than English. These factors need to be taken into account when selecting appropriate activities. In many cases it is possible to change a task, for example from a writing activity to a speaking activity. Most activities in this book can be adapted to higher- or lower-level students. You will find many suggestions for differentiation in the variations at the end of each activity. Remember to also consider your students' broader academic skills when choosing activities. Ask yourself the question: *Would my students be able to perform the task in their native language?*

Age

Each activity states the approximate age range that it is most suitable for. The 12–14 age group still has many of the interests and characteristics of primary students. The 'middle' group (14–17 years of age), are more independent and display many characteristics of adult learners. Most researchers also consider 17–20-year-olds as teenagers; however, in language teaching terms these students would be classified as young adults and hence are not specifically addressed. Nevertheless, the activities for 14–17-year-olds are in many cases readily adapted to young adults or can be used as they stand.

Time

Time can only be an estimate based on experience. The time suggestions here are based on classrooms of approximately 25 students. Please note that many activities extend over multiple lessons. You can follow the steps as laid out in the book or modify them according to your individual needs.

Beginner	Can use everyday expressions in concrete situations: personal details, daily routines, wants and needs, requests for information.
Pre-intermediate	Can express him/herself with some hesitation on topics such as family, hobbies and interests, school, travel, and current trends and fashion, but has limited vocabulary and makes frequent errors.
Intermediate	Can understand and explain the main points of a story or problem and express thoughts and opinions on abstract or cultural topics such as ethics, relationships, music, and films.
Upper-intermediate	Can give clear descriptions, express viewpoints, and develop arguments, using complex sentences and a wide range of tenses with good fluency.
Advanced	Can express him/herself clearly and confidently, both orally and in writing, with very few mistakes on all age-appropriate subjects.

Table 1

Aims

This heading highlights aims, often language items—structures, functions and skills—that are practised in each activity. In many activities, the specific language focus depends on decisions made in the classroom. In these cases I have not listed specific language goals. There is a greater stress on integrated skills work for this age level than in primary resource materials.

Materials

A list of all materials you will need to conduct the activity.

Preparation

Any preparatory steps that need to be taken: contacting a fellow teacher, rearranging a room, setting up Internet access, making photocopies.

Variations and Follow-ups

There are variations and follow-ups at the end of most activities. In many cases they are activities can stand on their own. Variations focus on different ways to teach the core activities, while follow-ups are suggestions for optional extra activities that build on the core activity. You will find many suggestions for technology integration in the variations and follow-ups. Some variations and follow-ups are really lessons in their own right.

1

Language-awareness activities

Bilingual studies show that strengthening students' skills in their mother tongue has a positive impact on second language learning.

While our primary goal is to encourage students to interact communicatively in English, it is also important to get them to think of language, not just English, as a system which can be analyzed and put into context.

For many people studying a new language, the entire grammar seems like one monolithic block without an obvious entry point . These students are frustrated because they don't have a concept to approach the new materials. Language-awareness activities help relieve this tension and the 'foreignness' of the new language. Promoting language awareness strengthens a student's ability to 'notice' similarities and differences and provides a focus to study.

The activities in this section allow students to look at language critically and reflect on its role in culture and across the school curriculum. Language-awareness activities have a positive influence on both fluency and accuracy by strengthening students' ability to inductively make decisions in discourse.

1.1 The archeologists

Level	Upper-intermediate
Age	14–17
Time	45 minutes
Aims	Various
Materials	Picture of the Rosetta Stone

Procedure

1 Ask the students if they know what an archeologist is. If they don't know the word, explain that an archeologist is someone who studies old civilizations through items and artifacts they left behind. Brainstorm archeological artifacts with the students. Some examples might be the Mask of Tutankhamun, or Stonehenge stone circle.

2 Ask the students if they have ever heard of the Rosetta Stone and show them the picture. Explain that it was an ancient stone which helped archeologists understand an ancient language. See if the students can identify any artifacts from their own culture with a similar significance.

3 Ask the students to imagine they are archeologists of the future. Tell them they have just uncovered a stone with writing from an ancient language known as English. The stone has only four words on it. Individually ask the students to write down what these four words are. They can be any words in the English language. Make sure that the students work alone and do not show their colleagues their words.

4 Place the students in groups of four to six, depending on the size of the class. Allow the students to share their words with their colleagues.

5 Explain to the students that they must now construct a story based on the words each group has. Thus, a group of six students will have twenty-four words to work with. All these words must be included in the text.

6 Give the group 20–30 minutes to complete the task.

7 Have one person from each group read the text the group has created. Note any errors in grammar or vocabulary and discuss them with the class after the student has presented the text.

8 Ask the students to speculate what a person from the future might learn about their culture from the text. Is the message unambiguous or open for interpretation?

Variation 1

Have groups swap their texts and correct them.

Variation 2

Vary the text type. Have the students write a poem, drama, or screen play, or newspaper report.

1.2 A shrinking sentence

Level Intermediate and above

Age 14–17

Time 30 minutes

Aims Various, depending on the sentence

Preparation

Prior to class, create or choose a long, complicated, difficult sentence and write the sentence on the board.

Example *Having studied all night and knowing that the test, like all the horrible tests he had taken before in his long and difficult academic life, would be long and difficult, Karl resigned himself to his fate, knowing, in the deepest, darkest part of his mind, that he would probably never finish college and go on to become a doctor like his father, his father's father, and generations of Bigelows before that.*

Procedure

1 Give the students a few minutes to read through the sentence and attempt to understand it.

2 Explain to the students that you want them to deconstruct the sentence by removing words.

3 Tell them they may remove one, two, or three words at a time. However, the words they remove must be consecutive, in other words, one after the other and not in different spots in the sentence. When the words are removed, the sentence must remain grammatically correct. Ask the students whether the meaning changes. If so, how?

4 Choose one person to start the game. Draw a line through his/her selection.

5 Ask the class if the sentence is still grammatically correct. If it is, choose another student to select the next word or set of words. If the students think a choice of words makes the sentence ungrammatical, ask them to explain why. If they can't, write the reason on the board next to the sentence.

6 Continue until the sentence cannot be reduced any further.

Follow-up

In small groups ask students to write their own difficult sentences to present to the class. You may want to give the students a topic for their sentences in order to contextualize the activity. Move from group to group and check the sentences for errors before continuing with the activity proper.

1.3 Proverbs

Level Upper-intermediate

Age 14–17

Time 45 minutes +

Aims Various

Materials Photocopies of Worksheet 1.3

Procedure

1 Ask the students if they know what a proverb is. Explain to them that a proverb is a short expression that describes a common truth or wisdom. You may need to illustrate the point by giving an example of a very common English proverb such as:

- *Actions speak louder than words.*
- *First things first.*

2 Discuss what these proverbs mean and ask the students if they can think of any proverbs in their own language which express similar ideas.

3 Divide the class up into groups of four to six students.

4 Hand out the list of 40 common proverbs to each group.

5 Divide the proverbs up between each group and ask the students to work out (or guess) what they mean. Give the groups 15 minutes to discuss.

6 Bring the class together and go over the students' answers. If nobody understands a proverb, explain it to the class.

Follow-up 1

Ask the students to research proverbs from other parts of the world.

Example *Never rely on the glory of the morning nor the smiles of your mother-in-law.* (Japan)

Gold coins to a cat. (Japan)

Do the proverbs tell them anything about the culture of the countries they come from?

Follow-up 2

Explain to the students that proverbs are based on customs from the past. Some of these customs are outdated today. Ask the students if they can think of ways to update proverbs for their generation. For example, they could change *Don't keep all your eggs in one basket* into *Don't keep all your data on one disc drive.*

Worksheet 1.3

List of proverbs

A bird in the hand is worth two
  in the bush.
A chain is as strong as its weakest link.
A fool and his money are soon parted.
A man's home is his castle.
Actions speak louder than words.
All roads lead to Rome.
All that glitters is not gold.
All's well that ends well.
Beauty is only skin-deep.
Better safe than sorry.
Birds of a feather flock together.
Curiosity killed the cat.
Don't count your chickens before they
  are hatched.
Don't put all your eggs in one basket.
Every dog has his day.
Fight fire with fire.
Great minds think alike.
Ignorance is bliss.
It is no use crying over spilt milk.
Let sleeping dogs lie.

Live and let live.
Look after number one.
Love is blind.
Money is the root of all evil.
Necessity is the mother of invention.
Never look a gift horse in the mouth.
Nothing ventured, nothing gained.
Out of sight, out of mind.
Practice what you preach.
Scratch my back and I'll scratch yours.
Still waters run deep.
The bigger they are, the harder
  they fall.
Time cures all things.
Too many cooks spoil the broth.
Two heads are better than one.
Two is company, three is a crowd.
Walls have ears.
When in Rome, do as the Romans do.
You can't take it with you when you die.
You can't tell a book by its cover.

1.4 Funny little rhyming couplet poems

Level	Pre-intermediate and above
Age	12–14
Time	25 minutes
Aims	Creative writing with rhythm and rhyme
Materials	Overhead projector

Procedure

1 Put an example of a humorous little poem made of four-beat rhyming couplets on the overhead projector.

Example *One day a man walked down the street*

With dirty clothes and smelly feet

He slipped on a banana skin

And hurt his hands and nose and chin.

2 Ask the students to describe the rhythm of this poem. Write marks above the stressed words to illustrate the meter.

3 Ask the students which words rhyme here, and write AA BB next to the lines accordingly.

4 Underline the rhyming words and see if the students can come up with alternatives.

5 Now split the class into pairs and ask them to compose their own poems with the same rhyme and rhythm structure. If the students need more support, provide the words for the end rhymes and ask them to construct the full lines.

6 The students read out their compositions.

Variation

Introduce other meters and double or triple rhymes.

Acknowledgments

I learnt this activity from Guenther Bedson.

1.5 Crazy gaps

Level All (intermediate and above for the Follow-up)
Age 12–17
Time 30 minutes for the simple version, 60 minutes for the Follow-up
Aims Parts of speech, vocabulary

Preparation

1 Before class, choose two texts the students will understand and remove ten words from each text. If your students are advanced, you can remove more words.

2 In place of the word, write in its part of speech, for example, *adjective*, *noun*, *past tense verb*, *preposition*; or its lexical set, for example, *animal*, *emotion*, *food*.

3 Photocopy the gapped texts.

Procedure

1 In class, go over the parts of speech or lexical sets that you have gapped to make sure that the students understand and recognize them.

2 Divide the class into pairs.

3 Hand one photocopied text to one student in each pair. Explain to the students that they mustn't show the text to their partners.

4 The student with the text asks the other student to think of a noun, past tense verb, etc.

5 Once all the gaps have been filled, the students take turn reading their new texts, which can be very funny indeed.

6 Hand out the second text to the other student in each pair, and they then swap roles.

1.6

Follow-up

Have the students create their own gapped texts. These can be very simple and common texts such as answering-machine messages, invitations, letters, short dialogues, or songs. *—(verbs, nouns, adjectives, adverbs.)*

1.6 Songs and jingles

Level Upper-intermediate and above

Age 14–17

Time 2 hours spread out over three lessons

Aims Translation (with varied structure and vocabulary), dictionary skills

Materials Photocopies of the text of a famous song or commercial jingle from an English-speaking country, photocopies of Worksheet 1.6

Preparation

Before class choose a popular song or jingle from an English-speaking country and copy the words on to a sheet of paper. The song or jingle should be contemporary and recognizable. You can find a large collection of song lyrics on the Internet (see Appendix).

Procedure

Lesson 1 **1** Divide the class into pairs and hand each pair a copy of the text. Give the pairs a few minutes to read through the text silently. Ask them to underline any vocabulary they don't understand.

2 Go over the words with the students. Point out any idioms or interesting collocations.

3 Explain to the students that sometimes singers or ad writers translate their songs and jingles into other languages. Ask if they can think of any English songs or jingles that have been translated into their native language.

4 Invite the students to share their ideas with the rest of the class.

5 Explain to the students that you would like them to translate a song as well, but this time you want them to choose a song from their native language and change it to English.

6 Ask the students to think about and choose a song or jingle for homework.

Lesson 2 **1** Ask the students to tell you what songs they have chosen. Write their choices on the board. If you are working with a monolingual group, you will probably have many shared choices. If your class has students from many different countries or language backgrounds, ask the students to explain the meaning of the title of their song or jingle to the rest of the class.

2 Hand out the translation worksheet.

3 Explain that some songs will have action, while others may describe feelings or pictures. Ask the students to identify the main points of their song texts. Ask the students to look for characters, actions, or images in their chosen song. Are there any details unique to their culture? Explain that they may need to change these images and content for an English-speaking audience.

4 Remind the students that when they translate, they must also keep in mind the rhythm of the original song. Explain that to keep to the beat they may need to change some images, but they should still aim to maintain the same meaning.

5 Have the students write down basic information about their songs on the song translation worksheet. Move about the room and discuss the worksheets with the students.

6 Assign the translation for homework.

Lesson 3 1 Divide the class into small groups of three or four students. Let the students show each other their songs.

2 Now have the students exchange their songs and correct mistakes they may find.

3 Ask the students to make a final clean copy of their songs or jingles and present them to the class.

4 Invite the students to sing their song to class. If the song is well known, have the entire class sing the song together.

Worksheet 1.6
Song or jingle translation

Name of song	Name of song In English	What's it about?

Photocopiable © Oxford University Press

1.7 Idioms

Level Intermediate and above

Age 12–17

Time Lesson 1: 50 minutes; Lesson 2: 50 minutes; Homework

Aims Understanding idioms

Materials Photocopies of Worksheet 1.7 cut in half and out into strips; student access to a library or Internet source.

Procedure

Lesson 1

1 On the board write the following two idiomatic phrases: *Hold your horses* and *It's raining cats and dogs*.

2 Ask the students if they can guess what the phrases mean.

3 Write the word *Idiom* up on the board. Ask the students if they know what this word means. Explain that an idiom is an expression whose meaning cannot be guessed just from the meaning of the individual words.

4 Ask the students if they know any other examples of English idioms.

5 Explain that every language has its own idioms. Some are similar to English, others are completely different.

6 Hand out the idiom paper strips. Ask the students to match the idioms to their meanings. Let the students work individually first and after a period of time continue in pairs.

7 Draw the table below on the board. Tell the students that you want them to think of idioms from their own cultures.

English idiom	Definition	Idiom in my language	English translation

8 Ask the students to find corresponding idioms in their own language and write them down, under the headings in the table. Ask the students to include both the original version and a literal translation, for example: German: *Du hast Schwein gehabt* could be translated as *You had pig!* If time is short, allow the students to complete the task for homework.

Lesson 2

1 Ask individual students to choose an idiom from their native language which they have translated into English and write it up on the board.

2 The class must try and guess which English idiom it corresponds to.

3 Ask the students if they can identify any idioms which translate word for word.

4 Ask if there are any English idioms that have more than one translation in another language.

Worksheet 1.7

Idiom	Meaning
He's got cold feet.	He's scared and not sure he can do it.
She's pulling my leg.	She's fooling me.
He's got a chip on his shoulder.	He's angry about something that happened and might get into a fight.
At the drop of the hat	Immediately, without having to think
Out of the blue	Unexpectedly
He put his foot in his mouth.	He said something embarrassing.
Beat about the bush	Not talk about things directly
Eat your words	Take back what you say
Face the music	Accept the consequences
Up the creek	In a difficult, almost hopeless situation
Spill the beans	Reveal private or secret information.
Turn over a new leaf	Decide to change your life
Bury the hatchet	Stop fighting
Kick the bucket	Die
Couch potato	A lazy person who watches too much TV
Once in a blue moon	Not very often
With flying colours	Very successfully
On the fence	undecided
Have a ball	To enjoy oneself
When pigs fly	Never
To give a piece of my mind	To scold someone
Blow your stack	To become very angry
Nip in the bud	To stop something early so it won't get worse
Get cold feet	To not do something because your are scared
Off the hook	Free of danger, blame, or responsibility

Photocopiable © Oxford University Press

Variations

1 If you have a multilingual class, create an idiom chart with corresponding idioms in each language.

2 Instead of finding translations of English idioms, have the students find English translations of idioms from their native language.

3 If you have access to the Internet, search for current English language teen slang as opposed to more common 'mainstream' idioms. You can find examples of slang on websites of teen magazines. However, be very careful to check that the slang is not rude or obscene. See the back of this book for some website suggestions.

1.8 English in the environment

Level Beginner and above

Age 12–17

Time Lesson 1: 30 minutes; Lesson 2: 50 minutes; Homework

Aims Vocabulary building, understanding the role of English in the world

Materials Photocopies of Worksheet 1.8; large sheets of poster paper (one per student group) and colored pens

Procedure

Lesson 1 1 On the board write a number of words used in English and borrowed from other languages. Some examples could be: *kindergarten*, *mosquito*, *typhoon* (German, Spanish, Chinese).

2 Explain to the students that English is so widespread these days that you can find examples of it in most languages. Ask the students if they can think of any English words or phrases in their language. Write some examples on the board.

3 Explain to the students that you want them to find examples of English in their environment. Explain that you can find English most anywhere: on a candy wrapper, on a street sign, in the evening news, in a popular magazine. Tell the students that sometimes English is used and it doesn't even make sense. Can they find any examples in their society where English is used in that way?

4 Distribute the *English in the environment* worksheet. For homework the students must record as many examples of English in the environment as possible, listing the words or phrases and the place where they found the examples.

Lesson 2 1 Divide the class up into groups of three to four students.

2 Have the students compare their worksheets.

3 Distribute poster paper and pens to each group of students.

4 Explain to the students that you want them to create a mind map of English in their environment.

5 Show them an example of a mind map, as in the illustration below.

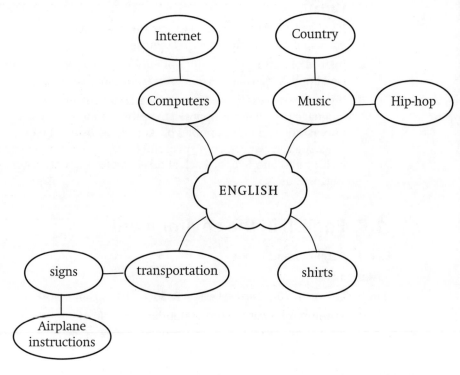

6 When the students have finished their posters, combine two groups and have them compare results. Have each group add any new information to their own poster.

7 Hang the posters on the classroom wall and let the students move around the room and see what their classmates have produced.

Follow-up 1

Based on the poster presentations, ask the students if they can identify any areas where English is particularly present in their culture. Can they think of any reason why this might be so?

Follow-up 2

Start a discussion about the pros and cons of the growth of English. Do the students think English hurts their native language and culture?

Worksheet 1.8

English in the environment

English word	Where it was found

Photocopiable © Oxford University Press

1.9 Street names

Level   Intermediate and above

Age   12–17

Time   Lesson 1: 50 minutes; Lesson 2: 50 minutes; Homework

Aims   Past tense, writing a short descriptive text

Materials   A map of an English-speaking city, such as Edinburgh

Procedure

Lesson 1   1   Draw a bubble in the center of the blackboard and in the bubble write *Street names*.

2   Explain to the students that there are very many categories used to name streets. Can they think of some? On the board write: *5th Avenue*, *8th Avenue*, and *Elm Street*, *Oak Street*, *Maple Street*.

3   Ask the students what categories of street names these are. Elicit the answer *Numbers* and *Trees*. Draw two bubbles and write the words: *Numbers* in one and *Trees* in the other.

4   Ask the students if they can think of other categories of street names, for example, special dates, famous people, landmarks, occupations, and so on.

5   Divide the class into small groups of three to four students.

6   Hand each group a map of a city in the English-speaking world. Two good options are Edinburgh and Washington DC.

7   Have each group categorize as many of the city streets as possible.

8   Move around the room and help students with vocabulary.

Lesson 2   1   Explain to the students that many street names tell stories about the past. For example, *Baker Street* tells us about what kind of shops were on that street long ago. *Washington Boulevard* is named after the first American president.

2 Tell the students that the street names in their town probably have a history too.

3 Explain that you want each student to choose a street from either their hometown or a city of their choice and write a short paragraph in English explaining the origin of the street name.

4 Allow the students to illustrate the paragraph.

5 Have each student present their paragraph to the class.

Variation 1

If you have good Internet access, ask the students to research the origin of a street name in an English-speaking city. See the Appendix for website suggestions.

Variation 2

Have the students make a Powerpoint presentation rather than a traditional pen and paper presentation.

1.10 What's in a name?

Level Intermediate

Age 12–17

Time 45 minutes (or more if the Follow-up is used)

Aims Verb *to be*, past tense, professions, dictionary work

Preparation

Prepare Worksheet 1.10 by writing a list of English names, such as *Carpenter*, *Miller*, *Smith*, *Felicity*, *Hope*, and so on. Mix given names and surnames.

Procedure

1 Explain to the students that different cultures have varying naming practices. In some cultures people have only one name. In other cultures the names can be very long. Give some examples.

2 Ask the students about name practices in their cultures. Put some examples on the board.

3 Give the students the *Names* worksheet and ask if they can tell you what any of the names mean.

4 Go over a few examples with the students.

5 Discuss why the parents might have chosen these names.

6 Ask the students to use a dictionary or the internet to find the meaning and/or history of the other names on the list.

7 As a group, discuss the meanings.

Variations

Don't limit the name activity to English names. As long as the activity is conducted in English it doesn't really matter where the names come from.

Follow-up

Once the students have realized that many names are tied to professions, ask them what new names might develop in the 21st century. For example: *Steve Programmer*, *Andrea Hardrive*, and so on. Let the students present some funny new names.

Comments

There are a huge number of websites dealing with the meaning of names. See Further Reading at the end of the book for suggestions.

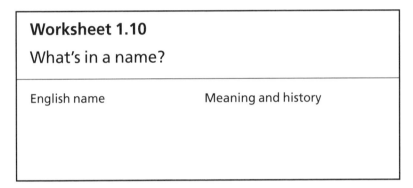

Worksheet 1.10

What's in a name?

English name	Meaning and history

Photocopiable © Oxford University Press

1.11 Repair English

Level Intermediate and above

Age 12–17

Time 50 minutes

Aims Rules of the language

Materials Coursebook or grammar text

Procedure

1 Ask the students if they think English is an easy or a hard language to learn.

2 Explain that many people find English a hard language to learn because it has so many exceptions.

Examples
- grammar: irregular past: *sing, sang, sung*; *bring, brought, brought*
- spelling: *knife, thought, bough*
- spelling and meaning: *wind* /aɪ/ and *wind* /ɪ/, *tear* /eə/ and *tear* /ɪə/.

3 Ask the students *Wouldn't it be easier to simplify English and correct its mistakes?*

4 Split the class up into small groups. Tell each group that they are in charge of rewriting the rules of English. They can change anything they want—grammar, spelling, pronunciation. As a group they must come up with three key changes they would make and present them to the rest of the class.

5 Give each group a copy of a coursebook or a grammar reference book to help them identify areas to repair.

6 Have each group present their changes to the class.

Comments

If you have a multilingual class, get the students to compare suggestions from various language groups.

1.12 Word association

Level	All
Age	12–17
Time	15 minutes +
Aims	Categorizing, vocabulary building; pronunciation

Procedure

1 Write a word up on the board, preferably a common noun such as *chair*.

2 Explain to the students that you want them to think of another word which is related to *chair*. Give an example such as *desk*. If a group calls out a word and the association is unclear, give the group one minute to confer and then ask them to explain the relationship. Accept wacky and creative ideas. Explain that if someone cannot find a related word, they are out of the game.

3 The students who drop out form a second group. The last player left in the first group wins.

Variation 1

The next word must start with the same starting letter as the previous word.

Variation 2

For beginners, let them use their own language and help them translate.

1.13 Sentence building

Level Pre-intermediate and above

Age 12–17

Time 15 minutes

Aims Vocabulary building; sentence structure

Materials Cards with the letters of the alphabet on them

Procedure

1 Show the students the cards with the letters on them. Put them in a stack and mix them like a deck of playing cards.

2 Ask three students to come up and choose two cards each. Write the letters on their cards on the board.

3 Divide the students up into small groups or pairs.

4 Explain to the students that you want them to write sentences using words that begin with the letters on the board.

5 Explain that they can also use other words in their sentences, but all six letters on the cards must be represented.

Example   M   L   S   T   H   F

Maria   likes   singing and   talking with   her   friends

6 Move among the groups and give help where necessary.

7 Have each pair of students write their sentences on the board.

8 The rest of the class looks for errors in grammar, spelling, and so on.

9 If the sentences have errors, ask the writers to try and correct them themselves. If they cannot, invite another student to come to the board and make the corrections.

10 Make sure that all the sentences are logical. If the students think a sentence makes no sense, they can challenge the writers to explain what it means.

1.14 Tongue twister competition

Level Pre-intermediate and above

Age 12–14

Time 30 minutes

Aims Pronunciation

Materials Photocopies of Worksheet 1.14 (see page 34)

Procedure

1 On the board write a common English-language tongue twister, for example *She sells sea shells by the sea shore.*

Worksheet 1.14

Tongue twisters

A flea and a fly flew up in a flue.
  Said the flea, 'Let us fly!'
  Said the fly, 'Let us flee!'
  So they flew through a flaw
  in the flue.

How much wood would a woodchuck chuck
  if a woodchuck could chuck wood?
  He would chuck, he would, as much
  as he could,
  and chuck as much wood as a
  woodchuck would
  if a woodchuck could chuck wood.

Three gray geese in the green grass
  grazing.
  Gray were the geese and green was
  the grass.

Of all the felt I ever felt,
  I never felt a piece of felt
  which felt as fine as that felt felt,
  when first I felt that felt hat's felt.

Betty Botter had some butter,
  'But,' she said, 'this butter's bitter.
  If I bake this bitter butter,
  it would make my batter bitter.
  But a bit of better butter—
  that would make my batter better.'

A Tudor who tooted a flute
  tried to tutor two tooters to toot.
  Said the two to their tutor,
  'Is it harder to toot or to tutor two
  tooters to toot?'

Peter Piper picked a peck of
  pickled peppers.
  A peck of pickled peppers Peter Piper
  picked.
  If Peter Piper picked a peck of pickled
  peppers,
  how many pickled peppers did Peter
  Piper pick?

Which witch wished which wicked wish?

Fresh fried fish,
  fish fresh fried,
  fried fish fresh,
  fish fried fresh.

Raleigh, are you already ready?
  Are you really ready, Raleigh?
  Raleigh's really ready, Riley.
  Riley, Raleigh's already ready!

Mares eat oats and does eat oats,
  and little lambs eat ivy.
  A kid will eat ivy too, wouldn't you?

The sixth sick sheik's sixth sheep's sick.

2 Ask the students to repeat the sentence a few times as a group. Then call on individual students and ask them to repeat the sentence as fast as they can.

3 Ask the class if they know the name for such sentences. On the board write: *Tongue twisters*.

4 Explain that most languages have tongue twisters. Ask the students to share some tongue twisters from their native language with you and the rest of the class.

5 Divide the class into two teams. Hand each team a copy of the *Tongue twisters* worksheet.

6   Explain to the students that you are going to have a tongue twister competition. Team A chooses a tongue twister from the worksheet. One student from Team A must repeat the tongue twister correctly. If Team A pronounces the tongue twister correctly, Team B must repeat it correctly as well. If they do not, Team A gets one point. If Team A mispronounces the tongue twister, they lose a point and Team B chooses a new tongue twister to pronounce.

7   Play until all the students have had a chance to speak.

Comments

This activity is a good lead-in to activity 1.15, 'Make a tongue twister'.

1.15 Make a tongue twister

Level   Upper-intermediate and above
Age   12–17
Time   30 minutes
Aims   Parts of speech, pronunciation
Materials   Dictionaries

Procedure

1   Review a few common English language tongue twisters with the class. If you have not done the *Tongue twister competition* (Activity 1.14), do steps 1–3 of that activity first.

2   On the board write the word *noun*. Ask the class to give you some examples of nouns.

3   Continue, writing *verb*, *adjective*, and *preposition* on the board and eliciting examples of each.

4   On the board write the tongue twister: *She sells sea shells by the sea shore.*

5   Invite the students to come to the board and circle the nouns, verbs, adjectives, and prepositions in the sentence.

6   Ask the students if these words have anything in common. Point out that all the words begin with the same letter and use similar but slightly different sounds. This is what makes the tongue twister hard to pronounce.

7   Divide the class into pairs.

8   Tell each pair that you want them to try and write some tongue twisters of their own. Explain that to do this, they must choose words from each category on the board and that all the words they choose must begin with the same letter.

9   Move around the classroom and help where necessary. Allow the students to use dictionaries or thesauri if they choose.

10   After 15–20 minutes bring the class back together as a group and invite pairs to write one of their tongue twisters on the board.

11 Have the class try and repeat the tongue twisters as fast as they can.

12 Take a vote and select the three best tongue twisters.

Variation

Have pairs exchange tongue twisters and edit their classmates' work for grammaticality.

Follow-up

Collect the tongue twisters and have the class create a book, poster, Powerpoint presentation or website. Allow the students to illustrate the document. If the students create a website, contact a partner school and make the tongue twister activity a school partnership project.

1.16 The world's longest sentence

Level	Intermediate and above
Age	14–17
Time	30 minutes +
Aims	Sentence structure, vocabulary building, error correction
Materials	Large sheets of white poster paper, enough for one sheet per group

Procedure

1 Ask the class how many words are in the longest sentence ever written in any language. Write their ideas on the board.

2 Explain to the students that there is great debate about this subject. Some say the longest sentence has around 800 words. Others report a Czech novel consisting of one sentence alone of over 40,000 words. Either way, it's a lot of words.

3 Split the class up into groups of four to six students. Explain that each group is going to try and write the longest English sentence ever written at their school.

4 One student in each group begins the sentence, then the other students in the group take turns to add words to the sentence. Alternatively, give all the groups the same base sentence to begin with.

5 Explain to the students that their sentences can be wacky, but they have to make some kind of sense.

6 Give each group a large sheet of white poster paper. Let them work on their sentences for 15 minutes. Move from group to group and read what the students have written. If you find errors, underline them but do not say what the mistakes are. If you want to give a hint, write either *spelling*, *grammar*, or *meaning* next to the underlined words or phrases.

7 When fifteen minutes are up, have groups exchange sentences and edit each other's work.

8 Have each group bring their sentences to you to verify the corrections are right.

9 Collect the sentence posters at the end of class.

10 Once a week, divide the students back into their groups and ask them to continue work on their sentences.

11 Repeat steps 7–9.

12 At the end of the semester (or any length of time you choose), have each group present their sentence. See which group produced the longest sentence.

Variation 1

Ask the students to decide which group produced the most complex, exciting or beautiful sentence.

Variation 2

Brainstorm sentence themes with the students, for example, weather, my life, school, holidays. Put the themes in a hat and have each group choose one. They must write their sentences based on this theme.

Follow-up

Once the long sentences are complete, have groups exchange their work and change the long sentence into a series of smaller sentences to form a cohesive paragraph. This activity makes a good lead-in or follow-up to activity 1.2, 'A shrinking sentence'.

1.17 My language, your language

Level	Intermediate and above
Age	14–17
Time	45 minutes
Aims	Grammar, pronunciation
Materials	Photocopies of Worksheet 1.17

Procedure

1 On the board write the word *articles*. Ask the students to give you examples of English articles. Write both definite *the* and indefinite articles *a, an* on the board.

2 Ask the students if their native languages have articles. If so, write them on the board underneath the English version. If a language doesn't have articles, ask the students how they know if something is definite or indefinite. In other words, ask them how they distinguish between an object or class of objects, and a specific object; for example, *a pencil / pencils* or *the pencil / the pencils*.

3 Hand out the language worksheet. Explain to the students that you want them to compare their language to English.

4 Review the language items in the left-hand column. Choose one language item, for example *articles,* and ask the students to write a sample sentence in English in the appropriate column.

5 Now have the students complete the worksheet with information about articles in their native languages.

6 Divide the class into small groups of four to six students. If you have a multilingual group, you can divide the class according to the students' native language.

7 Assign each group one or two language items to explore. Explain that you want each group to 'teach' the rest of the class about these language items. What is the same and what is different between English and the native language? Give the students approximately 20 minutes to fill in the information and organize their lessons.

8 Bring the class together and call each group forward to give their lesson.

Variation

If your group is monolingual you can turn this into a jigsaw activity. Assign each group an individual set of language items. When they have finished, pair up the groups and have them share their information, recording the information on their worksheets. Continue pairing and sharing until all the worksheets are complete. Invite each group to explain a language item to the rest of the class.

Follow-up

If you have a multilingual group, explore which languages are most similar to English and which languages are most similar to / different from each other.

Worksheet 1.17

My language, your language

Language items	Sample sentence	In my language

Photocopiable © Oxford University Press

1.18 Collocation cards

Level Intermediate and above

Age 12–17

Time 20 minutes

Aims Collocations

Preparation

1 Choose collocations from the list provided, or make your own choices based on what you have been teaching the students. You can also use a collocation dictionary for examples.

2 Photocopy Worksheet 1.18 so that you have two copies for each group of four to six students. Enlarge the worksheets. Cut up the words and phrases on each worksheet so that you have a set of 'collocation cards'. Mix the cards well.

Procedure

1 Divide the class into groups of four to six students. Give each group a set of collocation cards.

2 Deal six collocation cards to each member of a group. Leave the excess cards in a pile.

3 Each player looks at his or her hand of cards. The object of the game is to create as many collocations as possible until all cards have been used.

4 If a player has one or more collocations he or she places them face up on the table and takes a corresponding number of cards from the pile.

5 The next player lays down any collocations he or she may have and takes a card from the pile as well. If the player still cannot lay down a collocation, move on to the next player. Continue in this fashion until every student can make a collocation.

6 If a player lays down a collocation and it is wrong, the next player in line can complete the correct collocation with a card from his hand and keep the collocation. If this player does not have the correct card, the next player in line can complete the collocation. If no one has the correct card, the incorrect collocation cards are returned to the center pile, which is remixed.

7 Continue playing until all the cards have been used in collocations. The student with the most collocations wins.

Variation 1

Make the game harder and require each player to use the collocations they have collected in a sentence before they are awarded a final score.

Variation 2

Rather than using the collocation card worksheet, create your own collocation worksheet using materials taught in your specific classroom.

Worksheet 1.18

Collocation cards matrix

take	a break	break	a habit	break	a promise
break	the ice	break	the rules		
take	an exam	have	lunch	have	a bath
have	a look	have a	headache	take	a seat
get	rich	get	away	get	hurt
get	help	take	a taxi	put	off
put	out	put	through	put	on
give	help	give	birth	give	a concert
pay	a visit	pay	attention	pay	a compliment
make	a choice	make	an effort	make	plans
concentrate	on	decide	on	depend	on
rely	on	approve	of	consist	of
take	advantage of	explain	to	happen	to
matter	to	talk	to	pay	for
search	for	vote	for	wait	for
prevent	from	recover	from	subtract	from
suffer	from	fill	out	pick	out

Photocopiable © Oxford University Press

1.19 Silent scene

Level Intermediate and above

Age 12–17

Time Depends on the length of the film (60 minutes per lesson for the core activities)

Aims Creative writing, dialogues; speaking practice

Preparation

1 Choose a video or DVD that you think the students will enjoy.

2 Watch it and select a scene, 1–2 minutes in length, which has a fair amount of dialogue and is dramatic. Note where on the DVD or videotape the scene is located.

3 Set up the video equipment before class in a way that all students can see the screen.

Lesson 1 1 Tell the students you are going to watch a film with them. Write the title of the film on the board.

2 Ask the students if they have ever seen it before. If some of them have, ask them not to tell the others the story yet.

3 Play the video or DVD up to the point your chosen scene begins, pause the movie and turn down the sound.

4 Explain to the students that you are going to play the next scene without sound. Ask them to think about what the actors are saying.

5 Split the class up into small groups or pairs. Explain that you want them to create the dialogue for the silent scene.

6 Play the scene a few more times so the students can familiarize themselves with the action. Encourage them to take notes.

7 Give the students 30 minutes to write their dialogues. Circulate and provide assistance where necessary.

8 Have groups exchange dialogues and check each other's work for errors.

Lesson 2 1 Replay the silent scene to refresh the students' memory.

2 Tell the class that you want each group to act out their script. Give the groups ten minutes to prepare.

3 Make space at the front of the classroom and have the groups perform in front of the others.

4 As a class, compare the scripts. Did each group see the scene the same way? What were the differences? Would the scripts affect the outcome of the film? If so, in what way?

5 Play the rest of the film.

Variation 1

Just play a silent scene with no other context. The students create the dialogue for this scene and predict what happened before and after.

Variation 2

Chop a short TV show into equal sections. Have each group write a dialogue for one section. Then as a class, have them put their sections together. They need to work together to make their segments fit logically. Have the students perform the final outcome.

Variation 3

Play the silent scene while the students act out their dialogues. The students must try and speak in synch with the actors on the screen. This requires quite a bit of practice.

Follow-up

Film the students as they act out their scripts. Analyze the footage with the students. See if they can identify any mistakes. Go over any errors, especially of intonation or pronunciation. Then, let them make a second, revised version.

2
Creative and critical thinking tasks

In the first section of activities we focused the students' attention on language—how it works and the relationship between a student's mother tongue and the target language, in this case English. In doing so, the students employed a number of higher level thinking skills.

In this next section, we continue developing students' thinking skills, this time moving away from the topic of language specifically to broader issues. Here, English is the medium to solve a problem or create something new, as opposed to being the subject focus itself.

I have called this section *Creative and critical thinking tasks*. These can be elusive terms. For the purposes of this book we define the two terms as follows:

Creative thinking focuses on generating new ideas. Associated skills include flexibility, originality, and innovation. In other words: 'Thinking out of the box' or 'lateral thinking', to use a term coined by the psychologist Edward de Bono.

Critical thinking encompasses logical thinking and reasoning. Associated skills include comparing and contrasting, classifying, sorting, identifying cause and effect, looking for patterns, assessing and evaluating.

When an activity is designed so that it addresses both types of thinking, students strengthen valuable academic skills and stimulate their curiosity. For another book which appeals to both types of thinking, see *Global Issues*, in this series.

In language teaching, we need to be sure that we do not plunge into higher order thinking skills without setting the appropriate groundwork. More so than in the mainstream classroom, we must be aware not only of students' cognitive abilities, but of their language skills as well. In developing the activities in this book, I found it useful to use *Bloom's Taxonomy of the Cognitive Domain* as a guide and reference. It serves as a valuable framework for integrating critical and creative thinking, as well as developing broader academic skills. I also find the taxonomy especially helpful in differentiating learning for mixed ability classes. Below is a basic overview of the taxonomy. For more information see Further Reading at the back of the book.

Bloom's Taxonomy

Critical and creative thinking categories	Examples
Knowledge The ability to remember facts and information.	Choose, find, identify, label, list
Comprehension The ability to understand and explain ideas and concepts.	Conclude, describe, explain, interpret, summarize
Application The ability to apply knowledge to new situations. Basic problem-solving.	Construct, demonstrate, examine, experiment, organize, solve
Analysis The ability to break down concepts into smaller parts and understand their relationships.	Analyze, categorize, compare, contrast, conclude, deduce, infer, relate
Synthesis The ability to reorganize and re-evaluate ideas and apply them in a new way.	Arrange, construct, create, design, formulate, organize, plan
Evaluation The ability to evaluate and assess ideas, concepts, and processes according to established criteria.	Argue, assess, critique, defend, evaluate, grade, judge, measure, rate

2.1 Observe your world

Level Pre-intermediate and above

Age 12–17

Time 20–30 minutes, depending on level

Aims Vocabulary building; dictionary skills (in Variation 1)

Materials Coins or other common objects, such as bank notes or stamps, to describe

Procedure

1 Ask the students to look around the classroom and give some examples of what they see.

2 Write their ideas on the board.

3 Explain to the students that we often overlook many things in our daily life. We don't even notice them.

4 Take a familiar coin out of your pocket. Ask the students if they can describe what is on the back and the front of the coin. Most likely they will be able to identify a portrait or a symbol, but not much more.

5 Let the students look at the coin a bit more closely. If you have a large group you may need more coins. Point out details. Talk about how the coin feels. Is it smooth? Is it heavy?

6 Point to another object or feature of the classroom and point out its details, for example, a doorknob, or the wrapping on a candy bar.

7 Ask the students to move around the room and select an object or part of an object to describe.

8 Move around the room and give help where necessary. They will probably need lots of help with vocabulary.

Variation 1

Allow the students to use dictionaries to find vocabulary they need. In this case it could be better to have the students work in small groups.

Variation 2

Have the students read their descriptions. Their colleagues must guess which object they are referring to.

Comments

Coins have a habit of disappearing when used in a classroom. If your coins are valuable to you, you may want to consider using a different kind of object in steps 4 and 5.

2.2 Crossword puzzles

Level All

Age 12–17

Time 45 minutes

Aims Vocabulary building; devising clues and questions

Materials Overhead projector; sample overhead projector sheet with a crossword grid; photocopies of empty crossword grids; sheets of paper

Procedure

1 Ask the class to describe what a crossword puzzle is. Discuss briefly why people do crosswords. Try and elicit the benefits of crossword puzzles.

2 Display an empty crossword puzzle grid. Ask the class to give you the name of an animal. Write this animal into your grid and then block out the space at the beginning and end of the word.

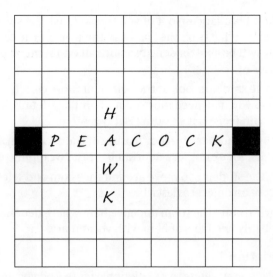

Photocopiable © Oxford University Press

3 Explain briefly how crosswords work and show how solution words are always interconnected in such a way that nonsense words do not appear. Ask the students for words that would fit and add these into the grid.

4 Show the class how to label the crossword grid with numbers for the clues.

5 Now ask the students to think of possible definitions that could form the clues to finding the solutions.

Example *A bird with bright and colorful tail feathers—* PEACOCK

6 Now divide the class into pairs or small groups of three to four students to make teams. Give each team a photocopy of an empty crossword grid. These should all have the same format, for example, 9 × 9.

7 The teams now have to think of English words to fit into the grid. The words should be from a theme you are dealing with in class, for example, nature and animals.

8 Ask the teams to think of clues and write them on a sheet of paper.

9 Once the crossword puzzle is complete, each group copies out their grid without the solutions.

10 The groups exchange crossword grids and clues and try to solve each other's crossword puzzles.

Variation 1

Concentrate on one particular language structure by requiring that all clues need to be either definitions, questions, or synonyms.

Variation 2

After step 7, have the teams exchange their completed crossword grids. Each team now has to devise clues for the words in the crossword of an opposing team.

Variation 3

You can make this activity into a competitive team game by awarding points. Award one point for each word included in the designing team's puzzle. Similarly, award one point for each correctly solved clue.

Comments

I learned this activity from Guenther Bedson. For more information about crossword puzzles see the book *Vocabulary 2nd edition*, in this series.

2.3 Color stories

Level	Intermediate and above
Age	12–17
Time	30 minutes
Aims	Writing from a prompt
Materials	Flashcards with colors on them, for example, a collection of paint samples

Procedure

Lesson 1

1 Randomly ask students for their favorite color. Ask the students why they like that color.

2 Explain that colors have a large influence on how we feel. People relate colors to moods.

3 Show the students cards with different colors on them. Elicit the names for the colors. If you are using paint samples, be sure the colors you select are natural and recognizable.

4 Ask the students to choose a color. Explain that you want them to think about how this color makes them feel.

5 Ask the students if they can think of a situation that goes with a particular color. Ask a few students to share their ideas.

6 Explain that you would like the students to write a story based on the color they have chosen. Depending on available class time, they can write the stories either in class or for homework.

Lesson 2

1 Ask the students to read their stories to the rest of the class.

2 Ask other students if they feel that the story was a 'red' story to them. If not ask them what color they think the story should be.

Variation 1

Split the class up into groups. Have each student in the group choose a color. As a group the students must now write a multi-color story. Have the group arrange the colors in the order they use them in the story and tell the story to the class.

Variation 2

Be more specific in your instructions. Have students write in the past tense, in the present continuous, in the first person.

Variation 3

Write a play, poem, or song instead of a story.

Example **A red and yellow story (angry and happy)**

Nina really wanted to see the Red Hot Chili Peppers at Madison Square Garden. Fuad said he would buy the tickets for her and meet her at the concert. The concert started at 8 pm. It was a quarter to eight and Fuad still wasn't there. Nina was angry. She was going to miss the start of the concert and not get a good seat.

'I'm going to kill Fuad', she thought.

She felt a hand on her shoulder. She turned around. It was Fuad. He was smiling. 'What are you smiling about?' Nina asked.

'Come with me', Fuad said.

They walked around the concert hall to a small door. A guard stood at the door. Fuad handed Nina a ticket. She looked at it. It was a backstage pass. She handed it to the guard and they went inside.

'Surprise!' said Fuad. Nina hugged him and gave him a big kiss.

They watched the concert and met the Red Hot Chili Peppers.

2.4 Newspaper lessons

Level Intermediate and above

Age 14–17

Time Lesson 1: 45 minutes; Lesson 2: 30–45 minutes

Aims Lesson 1: understanding a newspaper structure, discussing similarities and differences; Lesson 2: speaking, telling a story

Materials A selection of English-language newspapers

Procedure

Lesson 1 1 Ask the class if they read newspapers. Show them some English-language newspapers.

2 Explain some newspaper terminology such as masthead, headline, title, bi-line, column, editorial page, feature, and section.

3 Split the class into small groups of 4–6 students.

4 Give each group a copy of a newspaper and ask them to analyze it.
Write some questions on the board:

Does the newspaper have a motto?

How many sections are there?

What is the day's biggest headline?

What subject is discussed on the editorial page?

5 Ask each group to present their newspaper to the class.

6 Open up a discussion of similarities and differences between the newspapers.

7 Ask the students if they can guess who might read each newspaper. Why?

Lesson 2 **1** Ask the students to divide into the same groups as in Lesson 1.

2 Ask the students to browse through their newspaper and choose a story that interests them.

3 On the board write:

PEOPLE   PLACES   ACTIONS   THINGS

4 Ask the students to look at their chosen story and add information to each column.

5 Ask each group to tell their story to the rest of the class. Make sure that every student in each group gets a chance to speak.

Variation

In Lesson 1, if you can't find enough English language newspapers, use local publications as well. The students will still have to report on them in English.

Follow-up

After the students have recounted their newspaper articles, ask them to choose one of the people involved in the story and write the story from their perspective, for example, in the first person.

Comments

For more newspaper-related activities see *Newspapers*, in this series.

2.5 Shared drama

Level Pre-intermediate and above

Age 12–17

Time 45 minutes

Aims Process writing; story language, parts of speech; speaking practice (in Variations 1 and 2)

Materials Index cards in four different colors

Procedure

1 Split the class into small groups of four students.

2 Explain to the class that they are going to create a short skit in groups. The skit should last five minutes and all the students in the group must have at least one speaking part.

3 Hand each group sixteen index cards, four of each color. Give each student in a group one card of each color.

4 Explain that you want each student to write something on their cards according to the following scheme:

- *red = the name of a person*
- *blue = a location*
- *green = a verb*
- *yellow = an object*

5 Hand each group a bag (or a hat) and ask them to place their index cards in it.

6 Ask one student to draw out a red index card and place it on the table. Then ask another to draw out a blue card, another a green card, and another a yellow card.

7 Ask the students to tell you which words they selected, and give an example to the rest of the class. For example: *We selected Cleopatra, Los Angeles, swim, and comb.* Now explain that you want each group to think up a skit with the words they have selected.

8 Have each group create their skit. If you want, you can ask the students to write down the dialogue. Make sure all students get a chance to speak in the skits.

9 Each group performs their short skit to the rest of the class.

Variation 1

Rather than a skit, each group can write a story. The students in each group takes turns reading their story to the rest of the class.

Variation 2

Add additional colors and word types, for example, *orange = prepositions, purple = pronouns.*

2.6 What if ...?

Level Intermediate and above

Age 12–17

Time 45 minutes (or more for research in Variation 2)

Aims 'What if ...?' conditionals

Materials Photocopies of Worksheet 2.6

Procedure

1 Tell the students that you want them to think 'out of the box'. Write the term on the board and explain that 'out of the box' means thinking creatively and coming up with new ideas.

2 Explain to the students that you are going to give them a list of scenarios and they must come up with a prediction of what might happen if these scenarios came true.

3 Tell the students that you will work through one scenario with them together.

4 Write up on the board: *What if the world supplies of oil ran out?*

5 Ask the students to speculate what might happen. Write their ideas on the board.

6 Split the class up into small groups. Distribute the scenario list. Each group must choose a scenario and compose a short text (1–3 paragraphs) outlining what they predict might happen.

7 Students share their ideas with the class, either as an oral presentation or as a poster to hang on the wall.

Variation 1

Choose scenarios which link up with concepts they are learning in other subject areas at school.

Variation 2

Turn the activity into a research project, so that rather than simply speculating, students turn to the Internet or library to get facts on the topic.

Variation 3

Instead of a poster, students create a PowerPoint or a web-based presentation.

Worksheet 2.6

What if ...?' scenarios

What if there was no television?
What if animals could talk?
What if teenagers ruled the world?
What if man lived to 150 years old?
What if the North Pole melted?
What if humans could fly to Mars?
What if there was only one language in the world?
What if there were no laws in the world?
What if you won the lottery?
What if there was no private property?
What if you saw a beggar stealing food from a supermarket?
What if an asteroid hit the earth?
What if you could read people's minds?
What if you could become invisible?
What if you were born 500 years ago?
What if humans had wings?
What if it snowed every day for a year?
What if you could design a new city?
What if you were born old and life went backwards to zero?
What if we had eyes in the back of our heads?

Photocopiable © Oxford University Press

2.7 If I were king for a day

Level Intermediate and above
Age 14–17
Time 45 minutes
Aims Conditionals; future tense forms

Procedure

1 Write the title of this activity on the board at the start of the lesson and explain simply that this will be the subject of today's class. Look around for reactions. The idea might cause some smiling and giggling amongst the students.

2 Split your class into groups of five to six students. Tell your class that they should imagine they are in a position of power and they can make decisions to change things. Write some examples on the board:

headmaster of the school
town mayor
managing director of a local firm

3 Each group chooses a position and discusses what they would do. Tell them that the changes they make must be somehow beneficial, for example, for the teachers or students in the school, for the local community, or for the firm's employees. Allow only ten minutes for this.

4 Tell the students they must decide and write down the three most important changes they would make, and think of reasons to support these changes. They should be able to argue what benefits the school, town, or firm would gain from their proposed changes.

5 Have each group present their manifestos. Allow questions and discussion from the other groups after each presentation.

Variation 1

Have all groups take on the same role. This could be something with greater authority, for example, the President of the USA, or the Pope. Turn the presentations into debate groups, each group presenting and arguing their positions on key issues.

Variation 2

As homework, ask the students to choose a new position of power and write a short essay, stating three major changes they would like to make, and justifying their decisions.

2.8 Questions for the future

Level	Beginner and above
Age	12–17
Time	60 minutes
Aims	Forming questions, question words; note taking, summarizing, comparing
Materials	Small strips of papers to write names of groups on

Procedure

1 Ask the class if they believe it will ever be possible to travel backwards or forwards through time. Have the students justify their opinions.

2 Tell the class that you want them to imagine that it is possible to travel forwards in time just once. Ask the students: *What would you want to know? What questions would you ask?*

3 Split the class up into small groups of four to six students, making sure you have an even number of students in each group. Give each group a number or letter, for example, 1, 2, 3, 4 or A, B, C, D. Write the names of the groups on small strips of paper and place them in a bag or a hat.

4 Explain that you want each group to come up with at least five questions they would ask someone from a hundred years in the future. Give the students ten minutes to complete the task. Move about the room and monitor the language the students are using.

5 Bring the class together and have one student from each group read their questions. Write the questions on the board. Add a tick each time a question repeats. If possible, identify the top five questions.

6 Take the paper strips out of the bag two at a time, and pair the groups.

7 Explain that you want one group to ask their questions to the other. The second group must answer the questions as if they really were from the future. The groups then switch roles. Be sure that every student in each group asks or answers at least one question. Have the groups take notes on the answers to their questions.

8 Use the paper strips again to make new group pairings, and repeat step 7.

9 Ask each group to compare the answers they received to their questions. In what ways are their views of the future similar or different?

Variation 1

If you have a small class, this can be a pairwork activity.

Variation 2

Instead of the future, have the students travel to the past. This activity could be effectively combined with content from the students' history or social studies courses.

Follow-up

Add a writing component to this activity. Have each group write a short piece on their 'View of the future', based on their answers to their classmates' questions. The writings can be collected and put into a larger 'Views of the future' presentation. The presentation can be in pen and paper form, or created as a PowerPoint presentation.

2.9 The meaning of dreams

Level Intermediate and above

Age 14–17

Time 60 minutes (or more for the written task in Variation 1)

Aims Various

Procedure

1 Tell the class about an unusual dream you once had. If you can't remember a real dream, make one up. Say: *I don't understand this dream.*

2 Explain that many images in dreams have meanings. Ask the students if they can think of some possible meanings for the images in your dream. Accept all answers that are in good taste.

3 Ask the students to think of an unusual dream they can remember. Explain to them that the dreams can be unfinished or unclear. They should try and explain the dreams as best they can.

4 Pair the students. Student A tells his or her dream. Student B must try and interpret it. Student A takes notes on the interpretation.

5 Switch roles and have Student B tell his or her dream.

6 Mix up the pairs and repeat step 4.

7 Mix up the pairs one more time.

8 Bring the class together as a group. Invite students to tell their dreams and the best interpretations they heard from their classmates.

Variation 1

Make this a written activity. Have each student write a dream for homework. Collect the dreams and redistribute them to the class. Have the students write an interpretation of the dream they have received. After they have completed their interpretations, have the students move around the room and find the student who wrote the dream and give him or her the interpretation.

Variation 2

Ask students to interview their parents or friends about their dreams and then write them down.

Follow-up

This activity can be nicely combined with activities focusing on the role of dreams in society or history, such as Aborigine dream culture, or dreams and psychoanalysis. Obviously, you need to be very culturally sensitive when approaching these topics. Dreams are very powerful notions in many societies.

2.10 What would inanimate objects say?

Level Intermediate and above

Age 12–14

Time 60 minutes (less if the writing is done for homework)

Aims Writing a first person narrative

Materials A stone, cards with photographs or pictures of common inanimate objects, such as a chair, a floor tile, a pencil, a television remote control, a battery. You need at least one picture per student in your class.

Procedure

1 Hold up the stone for all the students to see. Explain that this is a very special stone. Tell the students that the stone was once a part of a great castle. The castle was the home of a king who ruled over a huge empire until he was defeated in a battle five hundred years ago. Say to the students: *This stone has seen a lot of things in its life. Imagine if this stone could speak. What would it say?*

2 On the board write the words *animate* and *inanimate*. Ask the students if they can guess what these words mean. Explain that something which is animate is alive. Something which is inanimate is not alive. Ask the students if a stone is animate or inanimate. Ask them about other items such as a tree, a window, milk, plastic.

3 Take out the cards with pictures or photos and distribute them to the students. Ask the students if the pictures are of animate or inanimate objects.

4 Explain that you would like them to imagine that inanimate objects can talk. What would they have to say about their existence? Tell the students that their objects can have moods and feelings too.

5 Tell the students that you want them to write a narrative story from the point of view of the inanimate object they have in their picture. Explain that they must write this narrative in the first person. Tell the students that writing in the first person means writing as if you were the person telling the story.

6 Give the students 30 minutes to finish their stories. Move about the classroom and offer help where needed.

7 Invite the students to read their stories to the class. Note any errors they make and go over them after they finish their presentation.

Variation 1

Collect the stories and mark them for the next class. Do not provide corrections, but give suggestions. Students edit their work either in class or for homework.

Variation 2

As a fun alternative, have the students write an email from their inanimate object.

Follow-up

Pair students and have them create a dialogue between their inanimate objects.

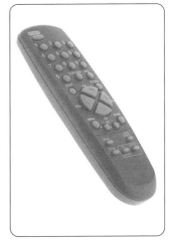

2.11 Rescue expedition

Level Intermediate

Age 12–14

Time 45 minutes

Aims Various

Procedure

1 Split the class into groups. Tell them they have just discovered that one of their best friends has been stranded on a South Pacific island and they have to organize a rescue expedition.

2 In groups the students discuss which items of equipment and which provisions they will take on the expedition. Tell them they are limited to taking only things they can carry. If they can't think of anything, suggest the following categories:

- Medical/Health
- Food and Drink
- Communication
- Transportation
- Shelter and Storage
- Protection

3 In groups the students plan their rescue expedition. They can reach the island by asking local people from the neighboring islands to drop them at the seashore by boat and to pick them up two weeks later. They need to think about the hazards they might encounter and make a plan of action as to how they would find their stranded friend.

4 In turn the groups present their list of equipment and their plans for the rescue expedition.

Variation

Give the students a choice of different scenarios. For example: their friend might be stranded in the Sahara desert, in the Antarctic, in the Amazon rain forest, on the Moon.

2.12 Sell a product

Level Intermediate

Age 14–17

Time 90 minutes (with additional time for the variations)

Aims Descriptive language, developing a persuasive argument

Materials Advertisements and pictures of internationally famous products; poster paper and pens for Variation 1; a video camera for Variation 2

Procedure

1 Show the students a popular product that is well-known around the world, for example, a bottle of cola from the USA, a Walkman from Japan, a model train from Germany.

2 Ask the students why they think these products are internationally successful. Why is it that some other products which are popular in one part of the world never reach beyond that region?

3 Explain to the students that products can become popular because of good advertising. Write the word *advertising* on the board and elicit its meaning from the students. Support the meaning by showing some examples of well-known advertisements.

4 Ask the students if they can think of any popular products from their home country. Write some of the ideas on the board. If you are in a multilingual class, ask students to tell the class something about the different products from their various countries.

5 Split the class up into small groups or pairs. Have each group choose a product to work on.

6 Explain to the class that they are businessmen and they want to make their product popular in an English-speaking country. What do they have to do? Elicit ideas from the students and write them on the board.

7 Write the following questions on the board to help the students focus:
Who are you selling to? What is your target market?
What is your advertising tool? Newspapers, TV, billboards, Internet, word of mouth?
What is special about your product? What are its features? What are its benefits?

8 In their groups have the students discuss these points and come up with an advertising strategy for their product.

9 Have each group present their advertising strategy to the rest of the class.

Variation 1

In the same groups as in the core lesson, have the students design an advertisement. Have the students draw the advertisement on poster paper and present it to the class. Alternatively, allow the students to design a Powerpoint presentation or web page instead of a poster.

Variation 2

If you have the equipment, let the students use a video camera to record their own commercial.

Variation 3

Show the students advertisements from English-speaking countries and ask them if they think the advertisements would work in their country. This variation works particularly well if you have a class with students from many countries.

Follow-up

For homework, ask the students to choose examples of advertisements (or commercials) that they feel are successful—the examples can be local or English-based. Have the students explain why they think the advertisements are successful.

2.13 The stock market

Level	Intermediate and above
Age	14–17
Time	Ongoing
Aims	Numbers, comparatives, prediction (*will*), past tense, present perfect
Materials	Photocopies of a stock report, photocopies of *Key features of a Stock report*, newspapers or Internet sites with stock market quotes, photocopies of Worksheet 2.13

Key features of a stock report

YTD % CHG stands for year-to-date percentage of change. In other words, how much has the stock risen or fallen compared to where it was a year ago on today's date?

52-Wk High shows the highest selling price of the stock in the last 52 weeks.

52-Wk Low shows the lowest selling price of the stock in the last 52 weeks.

Stock column gives the full name of the company.

Sym is the symbol used by the company on the ticker reports generated by the stock exchanges that track the trading of each stock.

Volume lists the number of shares sold (in hundreds).

Last shows the stock's price at close of business yesterday.

NET CHG shows how the price has risen or fallen compared to yesterday's closing price.

Photocopiable © Oxford University Press

Lesson 1
1 Hand each student a copy of a stock report and a copy of the *Key features* (see above). Ask them if they know what a stock is.

2 Explain that stock is the total value of a public company. A share is a piece of that total stock.

3 Tell the students that stocks are bought and sold at a stock exchange. The stock report shows how the value of stocks changes over time.

4 Take a company from the stock report and write its data on the board.

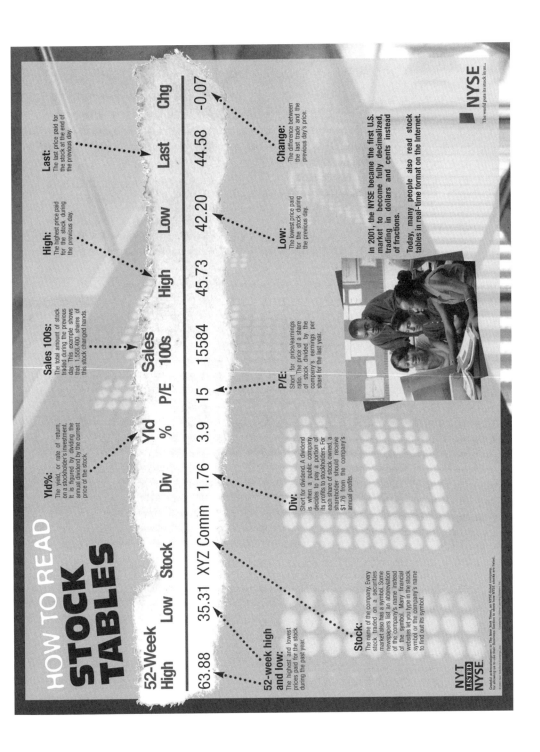

HOW TO READ
STOCK TABLES

52-Week		Stock	Div	Yld %	P/E	Sales 100s	High	Low	Last	Chg
High	Low									
63.88	35.31	XYZ Comm	1.76	3.9	15	15584	45.73	42.20	44.58	-0.07

52-week high and low:
The highest and lowest prices paid for the stock during the past year.

Stock:
The name of the company. Every stock traded on a securities market also has a symbol. Some newspapers list an abbreviation of the company's name instead of the symbol. Many financial websites let you type in the stock symbol or the company's name to find out its symbol.

Div:
Short for dividend. A dividend is when a public company decides to pay a portion of its profits to stockholders. For each share of stock owned, a shareholder should receive $1.76 from the company's annual profits.

Yld%:
The yield, or rate of return, on a stockholder's investment. It is figured by dividing the annual dividend by the current price of the stock.

P/E:
Short for price/earnings ratio. The price of a share of stock divided by the company's earnings per share for the last year.

Sales 100s:
The total amount of stock traded during the previous day. This example shows that 1,558,400 shares of this stock changed hands.

High:
The highest price paid for the stock during the previous day.

Low:
The lowest price paid for the stock during the previous day.

Last:
The last price paid for the stock at the end of the previous day.

Change:
The difference between the last trade and the previous day's price.

In 2001, the NYSE became the first U.S. market to become fully decimalized, trading in dollars and cents instead of fractions.

Today, many people also read stock tables in real-time format on the Internet.

NYSE
The world puts its stock in us...

NYT
LISTED
NYSE

2.13

5 Go over the columns *last* (the value of the stock on the previous day), *per cent change*, *volume* (the number of shares bought and sold), and *highs and lows*.

6 Randomly ask students questions about companies on the stock report. For example: *What was IBM's high yesterday? What per cent change was that from the day before? How many shares of IBM were bought and sold?*

7 Split the class up into pairs and have the students ask each other similar questions about companies on their stock reports.

8 Tell the students that you are going to run a stock market simulation. Each student is going to choose a stock and track it over the course of the semester.

9 Ask each student to choose a stock from the stock market report. Help students with the abbreviations. (You can find abbreviation charts on the Internet.)

10 Hand out the *Company profile* worksheet. For homework ask each student to research the company they have chosen on the Internet.

Worksheet 2.13

Company profile

Company name _____

_____

Company stock symbol _____

_____

Address _____

_____

_____

_____

Products _____

_____

_____

Number of employees _____

Sales in last three years _____

High stock price for 52 weeks _____

Low stock price for 52 weeks _____

Lesson 2 and subsequent lessons

1 Split the class up into small groups. Ask students to share what they learnt about their company with their classmates.

2 Hand out a copy of the day's stock report or ask the students to go online.

3 Have each student record changes in their company's stock price. Explain to the students that you want each of them to keep a graph recording their stock prices.

4 On the board draw a simple line graph. Label the vertical axis *stock price*. Label the horizontal axis *date*. Take one stock from the stock report. Say: *On October 11, a share in stock A cost $15, on October 15, one share cost $15.10.* Find with your finger the point of intersection of the date and price for each day. Then draw a line connecting the dots.

5 Each day (or week), have students check the stock market report and update their graph. In groups have students discuss their information.

6 If you have space, hang all the student graphs on the wall so students can read what their classmates have done.

Daily

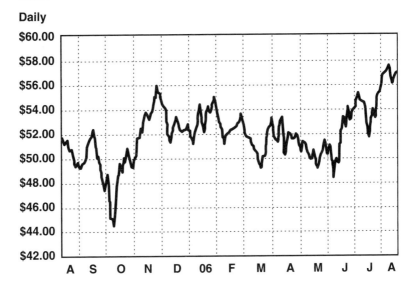

Variation

Rather than plotting individual graphs, hand out a larger sheet of poster paper and have each group chart their stocks on one graph, with each student using a different color. This will make comparisons obvious and easy to explain.

Follow-up

At the end of term ask students to discuss how their company did over the previous months. Ask them to think of the reasons for this performance. Did anything happen to the company? Were there outside factors—booming economy, war? This follow-up can be coordinated with a history or economics teacher.

2.14 Unanswered questions

Level Intermediate and above

Age 14–17

Time 1 hour spread out over two lessons

Aims Question forms; conditionals, developing an argument

Procedure

Lesson 1

1 Ask the students one the following questions: *Why do dogs stick their noses out of car windows? If a big liar says he is liar, do you believe him? If the universe is expanding, what is it expanding into?*

2 See if the students can come up with any imaginative answers to these questions.

3 Explain that there are many 'unanswered questions' in our daily lives and all we need to do is look for them.

4 Explain to the students that you want them to think of at least three unanswered questions and bring them to the next class.

Lesson 2

1 Split the class into small groups of three students. Have the students share their unanswered questions with each other.

2 Ask each group to pick one question to ask the rest of the class. The other groups must confer and try to come up with an answer.

3 Have each group write their own answer to their question in narrative form.

4 Give each student a job: writer, editor, idea giver.

5 Compare the answers and have the class vote on the best answer.

Follow-up

Collect all the student questions and make a 'Question book'. Include the answers. From time to time use a question from the book as a warm up activity, a closer, or an energy changer in your class.

2.15 The best excuses

Level Intermediate and above

Age 12–17

Time 30 minutes +

Aims Various

Procedure

1 Say to the class: *Once when I was in school, I forgot to do my homework. I knew I was going to get in trouble, so I had to find a good excuse.*

2 Ask the class if they know what an excuse is. Tell the students that your excuse for not doing the homework was pretty bad. The excuse was: *The dog ate my homework!*

3 Ask the students if they would believe such an excuse. (Probably not!)

4 Tell the students: *Well, maybe you have some better ideas.*

5 Divide the class into small groups of three or four students.

6 Write a situation up on the board and ask each group to come up with the most fantastic excuse possible.

7 Have each group present their excuse to the class.

8 Have the class vote on the best excuse.

2.16 Glass half full

Level Intermediate and above

Age 12–17

Time 30 minutes

Aims Various

Preparation

Prepare a list of 'ambiguous' situations, or use the examples on the next page. Photocopy the list so that there is one copy per student.

Procedure

1 Fill a glass half full with a liquid. Place the glass on a table at the front of the room.

2 Ask the students: *Is the glass half empty or half full? Raise your hands if you think it's half full.*

3 Call on a few students and ask them to explain why they feel that way.

4 Say: *You can see most situations either positively or negatively.* On the board write: *Even the darkest cloud has a silver lining.* Check that students know what this means. (There is always something good that can come out of a bad experience.)

5 Tell the students you have selected a series of situations. Split the class into groups and hand out the situation sheet, one per student. In groups, you want them to come up with a positive and negative side to each situation.

Example
- Situation: *I missed my train home.*
- Positive: *That train crashed. The next train was less full. I met a wonderful boy / girl on the later train.*
- Negative: *My parents will be furious. I'm going to miss my favorite TV show. The ticket is only valid for that one train.*

6 Ask each group to present the positive and negative sides of one the situations to the class.

7 Elicit from the rest of the class at least one more positive or negative side of each situation.

> ### Example situations
>
> Your boyfriend/girlfriend broke up with you.
> You just won a million dollars on the lottery.
> The new school year is here!
> You broke your leg.
> Your father/mother lost his/her job.
> Petrol prices have gone up by 20%.
> More people are immigrating to the UK than ever before.
> Your family is moving to another city.
> There was a power failure in the city.
> It's rained every day for the last two weeks.
> Today you are officially an adult.

Variation

Rather than working in groups, work in pairs. Have each student take turns being positive and negative.

Follow-up

Have the students role play one of the situations.

2.17 Map

Level	**Pre-intermediate and above**
Age	**12–17**
Time	**15 minutes**
Aims	**Directions, prepositions of place, geographical locations**
Materials	**A map of the world, small marker pens for Variation 1**

Preparation

If possible, clear a large space in your classroom or go outside to a playground or sports field. If you can't find a large space, see Variation 1.

Procedure

1 Hold up a map of the world and tell the students to imagine that the classroom floor is a map of the world. Point to the sides of the room that represent North, South, East and West.

2 Ask the students to shut their eyes and think of a place in the world they would like to visit, such as a city, island, region or country. Tell them not to tell anyone what place they thought of.

3 Once the students have thought of a place, say: *Now I want you to go to that place on our map of the world*. The students move to a space in the room based on the map of the world they have in their heads.

4 When the students have found their places, choose one student and ask: *Where are you?* Choose a few more students and ask them as well.

Pretty soon it should be clear that, in relation to each other's locations, they are standing in the wrong place.

5   Say: *There seems to be something wrong with this map!* Choose a student near the center of the room. Say: *Student X is in the right place. Let's get the map right!*

6   Encourage students to ask their classmates their locations. If you are working with lower-level students, you can write sentence stems on the board, for example, *Where are you? Are you in (Paris)?* Upper-level students can ask each other more detailed questions in order to get the map right.

7   When everybody has found their place, check the map for accuracy. Ask the students to point to North, South, East, and West. See if everybody points in the right direction.

8   If the map is still wrong, ask students what needs to change. Call on students and have them direct their classmates where to move. For example: *Maria, move to the left next to (in front of, behind …) Paul.*

Variation 1

If you have no open space available at all, you can play this game on a table. In this case, hand each student a marker pen and ask them to place on a spot on the table. Instead of moving themselves, the students move their markers according to the steps above.

Variation 2

Give instructions which require the students to use their geographical, historical, or political knowledge, for example, *go to a warm country*; *go to a country that has hosted the Olympic Games*; *go to a country that has a president as its leader*.

Follow-up 1

To check accuracy, add an extra step. Once the feel of the map is right, ask them to move again, this time to a place they would never want to visit. See if they can reorganize each other's locations correctly.

Follow-up 2

This activity opens the door to a discussion of geographical locations. Ask the students to explain why they chose a particular location.

2.18 Reporter at large

Level   Upper-intermediate and advanced

Age   14–17

Time   Three 50-minute lessons and homework

Aims   Conducting an interview; using information from an interview to write a narrative story

Materials   Photocopies of Worksheet 2.18

Procedure

Lesson 1   Interview

1   Ask the students if they have ever considered being a reporter. Tell them that to be a reporter they need to be naturally curious.

2   Write the word *curious* on the board and ask students to explain what the word means.

3   Explain to the students that you want them to become reporters for this project. The goal will be to write an article about someone they find interesting. This can be a neighbor, a relative, a teacher, or a local shop owner.

4   Explain that you want them to find out as much as possible about this person when he or she was a teenager.

5   Tell the students that they will collect information on this person by conducting interviews. They will then use this information to write the story.

6   Ask the students what kind of questions they might ask in an interview. Write some examples up on the board: *Did you like sports? Who was your first boy/girlfriend? Did you go away on holidays? Were you shy?*

7   Split the class into small groups and have each group brainstorm questions they might ask. Move around the room and listen in. Write some examples you hear on the board.

8 For homework the students must choose their interview partner and ask at least fifteen questions.

Lesson 2 **From interview to outline**

1 Ask the students to share who they interviewed for homework.

2 Say: *Now we have a lot of information. We have characters, settings, and events.* Write the three words on the board as column headers. Give out copies of Worksheet 2.18. Ask if there might be any other column headers they can think of, for example, *feelings, likes and dislikes.*

3 Individually, have the students write down information from the interviews under the headings.

4 Move around the room and ask questions, and give help where appropriate. Allow 15 minutes for this step.

5 Explain to the students that you want them to use their interview notes to create a narrative. Explain that stories have a beginning, a middle and an end.

6 Ask the students to write a story outline. Tell them to take the information in the top half of their Worksheets and try and place it at the beginning, the middle, or the end of their story outline.

Lesson 3 **Writing the stories**

1 Ask students to take out their interview/story outline notes.

2 Split the class into pairs. Have each pair exchange their notes.

3 Explain to the students that they will now write a story based on their partner's notes. Allow the students 30 minutes to write.

4 After 30 minutes ask the students to hand their stories back to their partners.

5 Have the students take turns reading what their partner wrote, adding details or correcting facts and impressions.

6 When the students are satisfied with the content, have them check their stories for language errors.

7 Collect the stories and hang them up around the classroom for the students to read in the next lesson.

Variation 1

Have students conduct the interviews in pairs or even groups and write their stories collaboratively.

Variation 2

Instead of switching the notes and having the students write about their partner's person, let the students keep their own notes and simply work individually in Lesson 3.

Comments

For more story-writing activities, see *Storybuilding* in this series.

Worksheet 2.18
From interview to outline

Characters

Settings

Events

Story Outline

Beginning

Middle

End

2.19 Poetry slam

Level Intermediate and above (pre-intermediate for Variation 1)

Age 12–17

Time Four 50-minute lessons

Aims Poetry; parts of speech; vocabulary

Materials Photocopies of various poems, one set of copies per group of students

Procedure

Lesson 1 Looking at poems

1 Tell the class that you are starting a new project. The project is called *Poetry slam*. Explain that a poetry slam is a poetry competition which focuses on both writing and performing. That means the students will not only have to think about what they say in a poem, but also about how they say it.

2 Split the class into groups of four to six students. Have them sit together around a table.

Place a set of photocopied poems on each table.

3 Tell the students that you want them to read the poems and choose one they like most as a group. Explain to the students that they don't need to understand everything to like a poem.

4 Ask the students to share their favorite poem with the class. Ask them why they liked that particular poem. On the board write: *sound/ rhythm*, *images*, *feelings*. Ask the students which aspect of their favorite poem appealed to them most.

Lesson 2 Write your own poem

1 Ask the students to get into the same groups as in Lesson 1.

2 Explain to the students that today you want them to try and write a poem as a group. Later, they will present this poem in the poetry slam.

3 On the board write four or five prompts, for example, *alone in a new city*, *lying on your back watching the clouds go by*, *growing up*, *a dark rainy night*.

4 On the board write the terms: *verbs, adjectives, adverbs, nouns*. Elicit examples of each to check that the students understand the terms.

5 In the same groups as in Lesson 1, ask the students to choose a prompt and brainstorm as many words as they can in the four categories. Move around the room and offer help.

6 Tell the students you want them to write a poem using the words they brainstormed. The poem may not be longer than two minutes. Tell them they will perform this poem as a group in the poetry slam. (If students are shy about performing, you can split the group up into writers or choreographers and performers.)

Lesson 3 Preparing for the slam

1 Explain to the students that a poetry slam has rules that they will need to follow. Write the rules on the board and go over them with the students. The rules are:

- *The poets can use no costumes or props. Music is not allowed either.*
- *The audience must remain silent during the performance but can cheer afterwards.*
- *One judge will be selected from each group of students. The judge will give the poems a score from 1–5. The criteria are: rhythm, naturalness, grammaticality, and performance.*
- *The scores will be added together and divided by the number of judges.*
- *If two or more poems have the same score, there will be a run-off performance and the winner will be decided by loudness of audience applause.*

2 Tell the students: *In the last class you wrote your poems. Now it is time to focus on your performance.* Ask the students: *What will you do? Who will do it?*

3 Split the class back into the groups and have each group go to a corner of the classroom to prepare their performances. Move around the room and offer help where necessary.

Lesson 4 The slam

1 Prepare the classroom space for the slam. If you have access to an auditorium or a small stage, all the better. Set aside a table for the judges to sit at.

2 If you like, you can have your class decorate the classroom or stage with a graffiti hip-hop motif.

3 Play hip-hop music as the audience takes their seats.

4 Acting as moderator, welcome the audience and call each group to the stage.

5 Collect the judges' scores but do not release them until the end of the slam.

6 When all of the groups have performed, reveal the results. If there are ties, go into the run-off round.

7 When a winner has been found, invite them onstage for an encore performance of their poem.

Variation 1

For lower-level classes, have the students perform poems by published authors rather than original creations.

Variation 2

Instead of using judges, allow the audience to judge each act by applause.

Variation 3

Assign an eager student to be MC of the event.

Comments

For more poetry ideas see the book *Creative Poetry Writing* in this series.

2.20 Usefulness of animals to mankind

Level Intermediate and above

Age 12–14

Time 30 minutes +

Aims Comparatives, superlatives, adjectives, prepositions; writing a short paragraph

Materials Flashcards of domestic and wild animals—one card per student

Procedure

1 Ask the students to make a line along a classroom wall.

2 Hand each student an animal flashcard. Elicit the names of the animals from the students.

3 Ask the students to line up according to the size of the animals. Ask one student to step out of the line and check that the order is correct. If it isn't, have the student tell classmates to move appropriately; for example, *Move the rabbit between the dog and the bird*.

4 Ask the students to line up according to the speed of the animals. This should be a little more difficult and lead to discussion. Ask various students for their opinions.

5 Tell the students: *Now I'm going to ask you something far more difficult.* Say: *Line up according to your animal's usefulness to mankind.* You can explain *usefulness* as something helpful to man—something that satisfies a need.

6 Allow students to rearrange their line. This should generate a lot of discussion. Monitor the activity and make sure students are talking to each other in English.

7 When the students have agreed on a line-up, call on the student with the 'most useful' animal. Ask the student to explain why it is the most useful.

8 Call on the student with the 'least useful' animal. Ask him or her to explain why it is the least useful. Ask the class: *Is it useless?*

9 Have the students return to their seats. Ask each student to write a short paragraph explaining their animal's usefulness to mankind.

10 Collect the paragraphs and select some of them to read to the class.

Follow-up 1

Have each student research their animal and give a short oral or written presentation to the class.

Follow-up 2

Instead of animals, use everyday objects.

Comments

This activity can raise contentious issues. Many teenagers are keenly aware of animal rights. Encourage students to state their opinions about questions such as eating animals or using animals for testing. For more ideas on using issues of wider concern in class, see *Global Issues* in this series.

2.21 Details

Level	Intermediate and above
Age	12–17
Time	30 minutes +
Aims	Descriptive language, adjectives
Materials	Paper and pens

Preparation

If possible, arrange a trip outside the school to observe a broader environment.

Procedure

1 Ask students to look around the classroom and describe what they see. You will probably get responses such as tables, chairs, blackboard, a map on the wall, and so on.

2 Explain that this is good, but there is more there than they might indeed imagine. Pick a detail somewhere in the room, for example, a stain on a carpet or the sun shining on a spot in the room. Describe the detail. Say: *Look at the stain on the carpet. It looks like a shooting star exploding.* Or: *Isn't it strange how the light falls on the desk in totally straight lines.*

3 Tell the students: *We often don't look at our environment closely. Let's take a walk and see what we can find.*

4 Explain to the students that you are going to take a walk outside the school. If possible, go to a park. If you can't, go to a quiet part of the school playground.

5 Explain to the students that you want them to observe their environment. Tell them to think like a zoom lens: they should observe things up close and far away.

6 Let the students work alone or with partners. Monitor pairs to make sure they are working in the target language.

7 Return to the classroom and let the students write up their impressions. Alternatively, you can have the students write their impressions for homework.

8 Ask students to read their impressions. See if the students share impressions.

Variation

Ask advanced learners to express their impressions in verse form. Have them write a poem about their impressions.

2.22 Who's stronger?

Level   Beginner and above

Age   12–14

Time   15 minutes +

Aims   Comparatives, superlatives, descriptive language

Materials   Index cards (20 per group), colored pens

This is a version of the card game *War*. In this game there are two players, each with a stack of cards. Each player takes the top card of their pile and places it face up in the middle. Whoever has the higher card gets to keep both. Play continues until one player has all the cards.

Procedure

1 Split the class up into teams of four students.

2 Hand each group a stack of twenty index cards.

3 On the cards ask the students to write either the name of an animal, or the name of a well-known hero/heroine from a movie, book, or action series. Make sure each student in the group writes five index cards.

4 Collect all the index cards from the groups. Mix the cards thoroughly and deal them back to each group.

5 Pair two groups together. Have each group lay their pile of cards on opposite sides of a table or desk.

6 Have one student from each team turn over the top card of their pile and lay it in the center of the table. Ask the students: *What (or who) is stronger?* Elicit opinions from the students. If there is disagreement, ask students to justify their opinions. If need be, you can act as judge.

7 The student with the 'stronger' card keeps both. Keep playing until one team has all of the cards.

8 Move around the room and monitor the game. Ask questions about the cards and encourage students to speak in English.

Variation 1

If you have a small class, play this game as a whole-group activity.

Variation 2

Have the students create their own card game. The students can choose their own criteria for the card value, and the rules remain the same.

2.23 Epitaphs

Level Intermediate and above

Age 12–17

Time Two 60-minute lessons

Aims Descriptive language, rhyme and intonation, poetry

Materials Photographs of gravestones, cut-outs of tombstones

Preparation

Collect examples of epitaphs. You can find hundreds of collections on the Internet. If possible find a picture of a gravestone with an epitaph on it.

Procedure

Lesson 1 1 Hold up a picture of a gravestone. Ask the students if they know what it is called.

2 Write the following epitaph on the board:

Here lies the body
Of Jonathan Blake
Stepped on the gas
Instead of the brake

3 Explain that this is an example of an epitaph. Tell the students that an epitaph is a short description of a person, written on their gravestone. Ask the students what the epitaph above says about Jonathan Blake. (He died in a car accident.)

4 Tell the students that epitaphs can be funny or sad. They can also be written from the dead person's perspective. The epitaph can be a poem or simple prose. The epitaph should describe the dead person in one way or another.

5 Say: *Here is an epitaph for a great teacher— me.* Write on the board:

Here lies teacher Gordon L
Man of great ideas,
Friend of all the students
Favorite of his peers.

6 Ask the students, jokingly, if they would write the same epitaph for you. Split the class up into pairs and ask them to write their own epitaph for you. Tell them that the epitaph must not have any rude language or be mean. Have all students begin their epitaphs with the phrase: *Here lies …*

7 Circulate around the room and help the students where necessary. Invite pairs to read their epitaphs to the class.

Lesson 2 1 Review some of the epitaphs from Lesson 1.

2 Tell the students that you now want them to write epitaphs for famous people they know. Explain that they can choose sports stars, movie actors, musicians, or historical figures, and that the epitaph should contain information about what the person was famous for or what people will remember him or her by.

4 Circulate around the room and help where necessary.

5 Hand out tombstone cut-outs. Have the students complete their epitaphs and glue them to the tombstones. Display the epitaphs in the classroom.

Follow-up 1

This activity can be combined with a history lesson. Have the students research famous figures and write their epitaphs. Similarly, students can take characters from books they have read and write epitaphs for them.

Follow-up 2

Take the students to a local cemetery and have them look at the inscriptions on the graves.

Follow-up 3

Ask students to research how epitaphs are written in their native language. What is the same as in English? What is different? Have the students translate an epitaph from their language into English.

3

Teenager topics

This section focuses on topics that are important or interesting to teenagers. However, rather than falling into the trap of trying to identify what is 'in' or 'cool' at the moment, these activities set up contexts which allow the teenagers themselves to provide content wherever possible.

3.1 Hybrid sports

Level Pre-intermediate

Age 12–14

Time 25 minutes

Aims Describing the rules of a game or a sport

Procedure

1 Brainstorm different kinds of sports with the class. Write a lot of examples on the board.

2 Now ask the class to try to define classifications for these sports, for example, ball sports, water sports and so on.

3 Split the class into groups. Tell them they are going to create a new kind of sport by combining elements of two or three different sports.

4 Demonstrate the following example:

Example Frisbee golf: In this game, instead of using golf clubs and a ball, the players throw a Frisbee towards a predetermined target such as a wall or a tree. Continue throwing from the place where the Frisbee lands until the target is reached. The fewer throws, the lower (and better) the score, as in golf.

5 Now have the groups discuss which sports could be combined and consider how a new kind of game might work.

6 Have the groups give their new sport a name and then present it to the other students.

Allow questions or even open discussion on whether the new sports would work.

Follow-up 1

Have students create a presentation of their new game or sport. The presentation can be on a poster, or as a PowerPoint presentation. The presentation can include illustrations and a description of the rules of the game.

Follow-up 2

If equipment and space allow, have the students actually play their hybrid sports. The English class could teach the sports to other students and have their own unique 'Hybrid sports day'.

3.2 Sounding off!

Level	Intermediate and above
Age	12–17
Time	30 minutes initially, and then ongoing
Aims	Expressing opinions
Materials	A bulletin board (either for post-its, or made out of cork to tack cards to), post-its or index cards

There is no question that teenagers like to complain about their parents, school, and life in general. They may even complain about English classes! Why not use this characteristic to your own advantage as a teacher?

Preparation

Prior to class hang a bulletin board up in the classroom.

Procedure

1 In a slightly over cheerful way, ask your class how they are feeling today. This should elicit some groans from the students.

2 Ask the students why they are groaning. Are they having a bad day? Write some of their comments on the board.

Examples *My parents won't let me go to a party!*

We have too much homework over the weekend.

3 Explain to the students that you know how they feel. Tell them: *You know what drives me crazy … ?* and mention some things that bother you, such as grading illegible papers, changing the bed linen and so on.

4 In pairs, ask the students to discuss what drives them crazy.

5 Point to the bulletin board on the wall. Tell the class that this is their 'Sounding off' board. Anything that frustrates them, angers them, or drives them crazy can be posted to the board. Encourage them to write in English, but accept, and then recast, ideas in their mother tongue as well.

6   Split the class into groups of four to six. Hand each group post-its or index cards.

7   Ask each group to come up with three things that drive them crazy and write them down individually on the cards.

8   Circulate, helping students to express their complaints in English.

9   When they are done, let them hang their comments on the 'Sounding off' board.

10   Allow the students to read what their peers have written. Let students write comments about anything posted on the board. However, make it clear that they must not insult people or mention anybody by name.

11   Empty the 'Sounding off' board at the end of the week and have the students post new cards.

Variation 1

If you are working with lower-level students, provide sentence stems to guide their writing.

Variation 2

If you have Internet access, this activity works wonderfully as a blog or part of a discussion group.

Variation 3

Instead of a board, use a journal, which you keep in the classroom.

3.3 Teacher's pet

Level	Intermediate and above
Age	11–14
Time	30 minutes (for the basic version)
Aims	Expressing opinions and preferences, explaining choices, describing people and animals
Materials	Pictures or photographs of common pets (various dog breeds, cats, birds, gerbils etc.), photographs of teachers, photographs of celebrities (for the variation), a photograph of your pet.

Procedure

1   Hold up a picture of a pet animal (preferably your own). Tell the students that this is your pet. Ask the students if they have any pets. Write the different kinds of pets on the board.

2   Hold up the pictures of animals and elicit their names. Display them all on the board or on a desk all the students can see. Explain that these animals are common pets in the UK. Ask the students if they can think of any other animals that people keep as pets. Do they have different pet animals in their country?

3 Hold up a picture of a teacher the students know. Tell the students: *Mr/Ms. X wants a pet too. What animal would you choose for him/her?*

4 Split the students into pairs or small groups. Give each group a picture of a teacher and ask them to decide on a pet for that teacher. Explain that you want them to give details to support their choice.

5 Give the students five minutes to discuss their choices. Move around the room and ask questions. Try and keep the discussion in the target language.

6 Ask one student from each group to present their conclusions.

7 Allow the rest of the class to ask questions and make their own suggestions.

Variation

Instead of choosing teachers, cut out pictures of celebrities such as pop stars, actors, or sports heroes and have the students choose pets for them.

Follow-up

1 Have the class create a pet poster with pictures of teachers and their selected pets.

2 This activity is a good introduction to a project on pets. Students can research celebrity pets on the Internet and find the most popular pets for different types of people. They can also learn about how to keep different pets—what they eat, how often they need exercise, etc.

3 Another option would be to make a pet survey in their school or neighborhood and present the results.

3.4 Name that celebrity!

Level	Pre-intermediate and above
Age	12–14
Time	1–2 hours preparation time in class or as homework, 30 minutes or more to play the game
Aims	Question forms; adjectives; past, present, and future tenses (simple and continuous)
Materials	Photocopies of Worksheet 3.4

Lesson 1

1 Write the following headings on the board:

Movies	*Music*	*Politicians*
Sports	*Television*	

2 Ask the students if they can name any popular figures from these categories.

3 Write the names under the category headings.

4 Explain to the students that they are going to play a *Name that celebrity!* game.

5 Tell the students that they will have to guess a celebrity by asking *Yes/No* questions.

6 However, first they will have to select a celebrity and research her or him.

7 Hand out the celebrity worksheets and ask the students to answer the questions for homework.

Lesson 2 **1** Ask the students if they have completed their celebrity worksheets.

2 Select a student and tell the class that they must try to guess the name of his or her celebrity. Tell the class they have a maximum of 20 questions they can ask.

3 Monitor the student questions. Make sure the questions are grammatically correct.

4 Once the students have guessed the first celebrity, break the class into small groups of four to six and have the students guess each other's celebrities.

5 Move about the room and monitor the groups, encouraging students to use only English.

6 Continue until all the celebrities have been guessed or until interest threatens to wane.

Follow-up 1

With the information in the celebrity worksheets, create a Hall of Fame to display in the classroom or in a book. Let the students illustrate the book or Hall of Fame with drawings or photographs from magazines or the Internet.

Follow-up 2

Ask the students to write to the celebrities. Many celebrity websites have email or postal addresses where fans can send their letters. See what happens if the students write. Do they get a reply?

Follow-up 3

Ask the students to play matchmaker and match celebrities with each other. Make sure the students explain why they think the celebrities would fit together.

Worksheet 3.4

Name that celebrity!

Celebrity name _____

Profession _____

Date of birth _____

Place of birth _____

Height _____

Hair color _____

Important events _____

_____

_____

Celebrity products _____

_____

_____

3.5 Timelines and biographies

Level	**Pre-intermediate and above**
Age	**12–14**
Time	**Two 60-minute lessons, plus additional time for research**
Aims	**Present and past tenses; sequencing words; writing a narrative story**
Materials	**Large sheets of white poster paper, colored pens, culture and teen magazines, computers with Internet access, a printer**

Procedure

Lesson 1   **1** Draw a timeline on the board and add the dates of important events in your life. Include information such as the year you were born, your first day of school, the year you got your first car, your first day as a teacher.

  2 Explain to the students that this is a timeline. A timeline is a way to describe events.

  3 Take a moment to describe your timeline to the class by writing sentences on the board.

Example   1965: John is born in Nassau, Bahamas.
1972: John enters school.
1983: John gets his first car.
1990: John starts work as a teacher.

4   Ask the students if they notice anything about these sentences. Explain that they are all in the present tense. Say that when we describe timelines in English, we generally use the present tense.

5   Hand each student a blank sheet of paper. Individually, ask each student to draw a timeline and include at least five key events in their lives.

6   When they are finished, put students in pairs and have them share their timelines with their partners. Move about the room and make sure that the students are speaking English and using the present tense.

7   After five minutes, switch the pairs and have the students share their timeline with a new partner. Switch one more time and continue to pair and share.

8   Arrange students in small groups of four. Explain that you want them to think of a famous person. It can be a historical figure, an actor, a musician, or a politician. Explain that it can even be a sports team— in other words, anything that has a history.

9   Tell the students that they will create a timeline about the subject they choose. They can research their subject in books or on the Internet. This research can be done in class or for homework. As in step 5, the students must include at least five events in their group's timeline.

Lesson 2 1   Ask each group to come to the front of the class and present their timeline. Make sure all students get a chance to speak.

2   Allow classmates to ask the presenting group questions about their timelines. Start by asking some questions yourself.

3   Tell the students that their timelines are very helpful if they want to write a story. Ask them what we call the story of someone's life in English. Write the word *biography* on the board.

4   Have the students return to their groups. Explain that you want them to write a biography based on their timelines. Tell the students that unlike timelines, biographies are written in the past tense. Write *timeline* to the left of the word *biography* on the board. Draw a line between them. Under the two words write *present tense* and *past tense*. Write a sentence in the present tense, for example, *John wins his first game*. Ask the students to change it to the past tense.

5   In their groups, students write biographies based on the information in their timelines. Move around the classroom and give assistance where necessary.

6   When they are finished, pair groups and have them exchange and edit each other's work. Have each group write a final draft of their own work.

7   Display the finished biographies in the classroom and allow the students to circulate and read what their classmates wrote.

Variation 1

Rather than writing a biography, have the students write an autobiography, using the first person.

Variation 2

If you have access to computers and presentation software, allow the students to write their biographies in the form of a presentation with accompanying illustrations or photographs. This is a good project to develop in conjunction with the school's technology instructor. If you have limited computer skills, the students can still brighten up their biographies by inserting art into a simple word processing document. (For more information on computer options see the section on *Teenagers and technology* in the introduction, page 10.)

Follow-up

From biographies it is a short step to drama. For students beyond the intermediate level, it is fun to take an episode from the biography and turn it into a skit with each group writing a 'screenplay' which they later act out for their classmates. See also *Storybuilding* in this series.

3.6 Soundtrack of my life

Level	Intermediate and above
Age	14–17
Time	Depends on class size
Aims	Various
Materials	CD player, or computer with CD drive

Procedure

1 Ask students to think of a film that made a great impression on them. Do they remember any music from the film?

2 Explain that the music that goes with a film is called a soundtrack. Write *soundtrack* on the board.

3 Ask the students why films have soundtracks. Explain that soundtracks help film directors create moods and highlight emotions.

4 Tell the students that you want them to imagine that their lives are films. What might the central theme of their film be? What kind of music would they use as a soundtrack?

5 For homework ask the students to think of a soundtrack for their lives.

6 In the following class have each student introduce their soundtrack and explain why they chose it.

Variation 1

If you feel choosing an individual soundtrack is too personal, put the students into groups and ask them to find a soundtrack to a movie on a broader issue, such as: *Growing up in …*, *Life with the parents*, *Schools and teachers*.

Variation 2

Rather than asking the students to choose a soundtrack, choose a song, play it to the class, and ask the students to come up with a story that fits the music.

Follow-up

Rather than asking the students to choose one soundtrack, have them make a 'sampler' with portions of songs representing different stages or events in their lives. This sampler can be combined with a Powerpoint presentation to create an audio-visual experience.

3.7 What happened to you?

Level Beginner and above

Age 12–17

Time 45 minutes

Aim Past tense, time expressions, writing an email

Materials Copy of an email to an old friend

Procedure

1 Tell your students that you recently received an email from an old college friend. In the email, your friend told you about his life since you last saw each other. Make up something dramatic. Tell your students: *Imagine, crazy Jim from college is now president of a bank!*

2 Ask the students if they can remember any old friends from kindergarten. Ask what they would say to them after all these years. What would they want to know? Write some of their ideas on the board.

3 Explain to the students that you want them to write an email to an old friend from kindergarten. In the email the students should tell their old friend what has happened in their life since they last met. Tell the students that they can choose to tell the true story of their life or make up something fun and dramatic.

4 Ask the students if their email should be formal or informal. Explain that an email to a friend is almost like talking to them. The language should be chatty and relaxed. Remind them that they are writing to a real person they once knew.

5 Move around the room and help the students where necessary.

6 When the students have finished their emails, invite them to share them with the rest of the class. Ask them to tell the class a little bit about the person they are writing to before reading their email.

Variation

For beginners provide sentence stems, for example, time expressions, such as *last year, three years ago*, etc. You can also create a gapped email text which the students complete with their own information.

Extension

Have students really contact old friends. They needn't be from kindergarten, but can be from any time in their life. They key is that they haven't spoken for quite some time.

3.8 Make a recipe

Level	Pre- intermediate
Age	12–14
Time	30 minutes
Aims	Imperatives
Materials	25–30 flashcards with items of food / ingredients for recipes

Procedure

1 Use the flashcards to review the vocabulary of food items and hang the cards up on the board. If you like, have the students attempt to categorize ingredients.

2 Split the class into groups. Tell them they are going to make a recipe for a new dish. They may choose a maximum of ten ingredients.

3 The groups discuss what kind of dish they want to invent and list their ingredients.

4 Now have the groups discuss which kitchen utensils or pieces of cooking equipment they require to prepare the dish. Help with new vocabulary where required.

5 Finally have each group write a step-by-step recipe using imperatives.

Variation

If you have a multicultural group, have the class create an international cookbook. If you want to get really creative, you can have the students actually cook the recipes and have an international food fair, either for their own class or for the school in general.

3.9 Life game

Level Pre-intermediate and above (depending on how closely you structure the input)

Age 12–17

Time 45 minutes

Aims Describing events, simple past

Materials For each group of six students: a large sheet of white poster paper, one dice, 1 colored counter per student, 5 small index cards per student

Procedure

1 Split the class into groups of six students and give each group a large sheet of white poster paper, a dice, a counter for each student, and five small index cards per student.

2 Tell the group to draw a track on the poster board with 65 squares, which they then number from 1–65.

3 Instruct the students to draw a 'start' space before square one and write in the word *Birth* and a 'finish' space after square 65 and here write in the word *Retirement*. This is now the playing board for the *Life game*.

4 Explain to the students that the board is a timeline of their lives from birth to retirement. Each square represents a year in their lives; the number is their age.

5 Ask the students to think of events that might take place during their lives at a certain age.

6 On the back of each index card they should write five different numbers (or ages). The students may choose any numbers from 1–65. Tell the students not to duplicate each other's numbers, so that the cards represent different ages.

7 Ask the students to think of events that might happen at the ages in life they have chosen.

8 The students write a short description of each event on the front of their cards. The first time you make this game, you could tell the students to choose only positive events.

Examples
- Age 4: You get a bicycle for your birthday.
- Age 18: You pass your high school exams.
- Age 25: You get married.
- Age 42: You get promoted to managing director.
- Age 62: Your first grandchild is born.

9 Now each group can play the board game. In turn students roll the dice and move their counter along the track. When they land on a square, all the students in the group check to see if they have a card representing that age. If so, they read out the event and pass the card over to the player.

10 Eventually all of the students will reach retirement. In turn, they can now recount their 'life', by retelling the events on the cards they collected using the simple past.

Variation 1

Have the students mix in some negative events.

Examples
- Age 8: You fail a math test in school.
- Age 32: You lose your job.
- Age 43: You get divorced.

Variation 2

After the game has ended, ask the students to imagine how things might have turned out differently if they had made different choices. This is a good context for practicing the conditional. For example: *If I had stayed in the UK, I would speak fluent English today.*

Acknowledgments

Many thanks to Guenther Bedson for contributing to the final version of this activity.

3.10 Holidays and festivals

Level Pre-intermediate and above (beginner in Variation 2)
Age 12–14
Time 60 minutes
Aims Describing an event
Materials White paper, color pens, computers for Follow-up

Procedure

1 Ask the students for their favorite holidays and festivals. Write their ideas on the board.

2 Explain to the students that the same holiday is often celebrated differently from country to country.

3 Write *New Year* on the board. Elicit how that holiday is celebrated in their countries. Is it celebrated in the same way, for example, in the UK?

4 Ask the students why we celebrate holidays. (Historical events, famous people, religious reasons.)

5 See if the students can name at least one holiday from each category.

6 Tell the students that you want them to create their own new holidays now.

7 Ask them to think about the following:
- What does the holiday celebrate? (person, event)
- What do you do on this holiday?
- What day is the holiday?

8 Give each student a sheet of white paper and ask them to write down their ideas. Allow students to illustrate their pages as well.

Variation 1

In step 6 have the students make a multicultural holiday calendar. See if the students can draw any conclusions from the calendar. (Which month has most or least holidays? How many holidays are religious? or historical?)

Variation 2

For beginners provide sentence stems such as:
- My holiday's name is …
- My holiday celebrates …
- My holiday is on …

Follow-up

Have the students create a holiday calendar or holiday book with their newly created holidays. If you have access to computer technology and the skills to create a simple website or presentation (or maybe a colleague knows how and can help you), you can create a calendar where each date with a holiday is a hotlink, opening up to a holiday page with information about the student's holiday and any art or photos they wish to add.

3.11 Martian law

Level	Intermediate and above
Age	12–17
Time	60 minutes
Aims	Various
Materials	Photocopies of Worksheet 3.11

Procedure

1 Explain to the students that you want them to imagine a situation in the future. Humans have met aliens and together with them have established a settlement on Mars. The new settlers are meeting for the first time to create a constitution for their Martian settlement.

2 Ask the students to think about the word *rights*. What does it mean? Give them some examples to think about, for example, *Is having a house to live in a right? Is it a right to read any book you want?*

3 Split the students up into small groups. Ask each group to come up with five rights for the Martian settlement. Have each group present these rights to the class. Write the rights on the board. Put a check mark next to rights that have already been suggested.

4 Explain to the students that it is important to have rights, but people must also have responsibilities if these rights are to be guaranteed. Pick a right and brainstorm with the students what responsibilities each citizen has in order to guarantee this right.

5 As a class, the students agree on five core rights and responsibilities for the new settlement and write them on the worksheet.

Variations

Instead of Martian law, create laws for the language classroom. This may be more appropriate for the older teenagers who might find the Martian concept 'childish'. It also has the added benefit of establishing your classroom rules.

Follow-up 1

Ask the students to think about the rights and responsibilities of teenagers (up to the age of 18 or whatever age one becomes a legal adult in that country). Discuss questions such as:

- Should teenagers go to jail for a crime?
- Do teenagers have the right to live by themselves?

Follow-up 2

Elicit other questions from the students and create a teenage Bill of Rights.

Comments

This activity can be very controversial (and political). As a teacher you will need to tailor the discussions to your local realities. Be careful, especially if you are not native to the country where you teach, not to force your own agenda on the students. This could create difficulties for you and the students themselves.

Worksheet 3.11

Martian law

Rights	Responsibilities

3.12 Save the Earth

Level Intermediate

Age 12–17

Time 30 minutes

Aims Cause and effect sentences; environment vocabulary

Materials A map of the world or globe, photographs of pollution and environmental problems (optional)

Procedure

1 Say to the students: *The world's temperature is rising. Why is this?* In a box on the right side of the board write *Global warming*. On the left side of the board draw an empty box. Ask students for their ideas about the causes of global warming (for example, factory smoke, car exhausts) and write them in the box.

2 Explain that factory smoke and car exhausts are causes of global warming. Write *cause* underneath the left-hand box. Underneath the global warming box write *effect*. Explain that the temperature is getting warmer because of factory smoke and car exhausts. Say: *Factory smoke is a cause and global warming is an effect.*

3 Say to the students: *The Earth is not healthy!* Ask them if they can think of any other environmental problems. Write them on the board in the right-hand box.

4 Split the class up into groups. Have each group select an environmental problem. Each group brainstorms the causes of the problem and suggests things people can do to prevent it.

5 Each group presents their findings to the class. Invite students to suggest additional steps they can take to preserve the environment.

Variation 1

Instead of a problem, have the students pick a part of the world and investigate its environmental challenges. This activity can be combined with geography or social studies activities.

Variation 2

The students investigate their town, region, or country and identify its environmental problems and propose possible solutions.

Comments

For more activities on similar topics, see *Global Issues* in this series, which also includes numerous sources of information.

3.13 The next big trend

Level Intermediate and above

Age 12–17

Time 30 minutes

Aims Rhetorical phrases such as *I think … In my opinion … We believe …* ; future tenses (*will* and *going to*); conditional (*could be*); past tense (for Follow-up 2)

Procedure

1 Tell the students: *Imagine you are the editor of an important youth magazine. Your boss has told you to write an article on the next big trend. What will it be?*

2 Explain that there can be different trends in different areas: music, sports, art, clothes, hairstyles, technology and so on.

3 Split the class up into small groups.

4 Have each group choose one area to explore and find a new trend.

5 Give the students 15 minutes to brainstorm their new trend.

6 Ask each group to present their findings to the class.

7 Have the class vote on the coolest new trend.

Follow-up 1

Ask the students to talk about what the current big trends are.

Follow-up 2

Have the students think back to previous generations. Ask them to tell you what was trendy in the 1960s, 1970s or 1980s.

Follow-up 3

Collaborate with a history teacher and have the students research trends from a hundred, two hundred or three hundred years ago.

3.14 Monuments and memorials

Level Intermediate and above

Age 12–17

Time 60 minutes

Aims Writing a descriptive text

Materials Photographs of famous monuments, statues, or memorials (local or international); photocopies of Worksheet 3.14

Procedure

1 Hold up a photograph of a famous memorial the students will recognize, and ask them what person or event it commemorates.

Memorial to Crazy Horse, South Dakota, USA

Taj Mahal, Agra, India: the tomb of Mumtaz Mahal

Statue of Abraham Lincoln, Washington, DC, USA

Vietnam War Veterans' Memorial, Washington, DC, USA

2 Ask the students why the person or event is worth commemorating. Say: *Surely, there are other people or events you would commemorate as well.*

3 Tell the students: *I want you to design a statue or memorial to a person or event that is important to teenagers.*

4 Hand out the memorial worksheet. Ask the students to answer the questions.

5 Walk around the room and talk to individual students as they fill out the questions on the memorial worksheet.

Worksheet 3.14

Teenage memorial

Name of the memorial:

What does the memorial honor?
- [ ] Person
- [ ] Event
- [ ] Place
- [ ] Other

Explain:

Are there any words on the memorial?

Location:	Size:
Materials:	Date:

Picture:

Description:

6   Ask the students to draw a picture of their memorial in the space on the page.

7   Finally, ask the students to write a paragraph about their memorial using the information from the questions they have just answered, in the order it appears on the worksheet.

8   Split the class into pairs and have the students exchange their worksheets with their partners.

9   Each partner checks the description on the worksheet for language errors and asks any questions they may have about the content.

10   Students then retrieve their own worksheets and write a final version of the paragraph.

Variation

This can also be done as a group work activity.

Follow-up 1

Have the students research existing memorials and statues on the Internet, and ask them to report back to the class about them.

Follow-up 2

If the local culture permits, discuss the history behind famous memorials. Ask the students if they think it is right to celebrate these people or events.

Follow-up 3

Ask the students to give a short presentation on their memorials to the class.

3.15 Teen alphabet book

Level Beginner and above

Age 12–14

Time Lesson 1: 50 minutes; Lesson 2: 30 minutes (or more depending on class size)

Aims Vocabulary building

Materials White poster paper (1 sheet per group of 4–6 students), colored pens, lots of magazines to cut out pictures from, glue, an alphabet book as an example

Procedure

Lesson 1 1   Hold up a children's alphabet book (either in English or another language). Ask the students if they remember such a book from their childhood.

2 Tell the students that alphabet books don't only have to be for children. Explain that you could also write one for adults.

Examples *'B' is for bills that have to be paid.*
'W' is for work where I go every day.

3 Say: *I want you to write an alphabet poster for teenagers!*

4 Tell the students that they must use the form *'Letter' is for …* in their posters.

5 Split the class into small groups of four to six students.

6 Have the students sit around a large table. Distribute poster paper, pens, magazines, and glue to each group.

7 Explain to the students that they can decorate their posters with pictures from the magazines or their own drawings.

8 Move around the room and offer help where appropriate. Ask the students to explain some of the choices they made—you may not know what they mean!

Lesson 2 1 Hang the posters on the classroom wall or prop them up on the board. Let the students get up and walk around and look at what their classmates came up with.

2 Ask each group to present their alphabet poster. Each student in the group can read a few letters.

3 Discuss the posters with the class. What similarities can they find? Is there anything on one poster that you can't find on any others?

4 Pick a few particularly interesting and/or controversial excerpts from the posters and initiate a class discussion on the subject; for example, *'B' is for bullies who push me around.*

Variation 1

Ask each group to choose a particular subject that interests them and make an alphabet poster on this.

Variation 2

Instead of a poster, have the students make a Powerpoint presentation or webpage. They can illustrate the page by cutting and pasting pictures from the Internet.

Comments

Although this activity targets the lower age group, many older teenagers really enjoy it. Older teenagers tend to look at this activity humorously, something I suggest encouraging, within the boundaries of good taste.

3.16 Anti-rules

Level Pre-intermediate and above

Age 12–17

Time 30 minutes +

Aims Imperatives; superlatives; negation; antonyms

Procedure

1 Ask the students to think of the five most important school rules.

2 Invite students to tell you one or two of their choices and write them on the board.

3 Say: *These are very good choices, but what if you wanted to get in trouble all the time? You would probably do the opposite of what we wrote down.*

4 On the board write: *Anti-rules.*

5 Choose a rule from the board, for example: *Do not eat in class.* The students create an anti-rule: *Always eat in class.*

6 Try a second rule which does not have an obvious opposite.

Example • Raise your hand if you have a question.

Elicit some ideas from the students.

Examples • Interrupt when you have a question.

• Call out when you have a question.

7 On the board write the following situations (or others of your choice):

• Learning a foreign language

• Being a successful student

• Being a good athlete

• Meeting a girlfriend/boyfriend

8 Split the class up into small groups and ask each group to come up with a set of anti-rules for each situation. Explain to the students that you obviously need to have an idea of what the real rules are to make up anti-rules.

9 Once the students have completed their anti-rules, ask each group to present them to the class. Write the anti-rules on the board as they speak.

10 Let the class suggest additional anti-rules to add to the list.

11 See if the students can guess the 'real rule' behind each anti-rule.

Variation

If you have a large class, instead of having groups present to the whole class, create pairs of groups and have each group try and guess the real rule behind the other's anti-rules.

3.17 Gapping songs

Level	Intermediate and above
Age	12–17
Time	15 minutes +
Aims	Listening skills; vocabulary building
Materials	CDs and CD player (or other device for playing music)

English language music is popular around the world and many people claim to know the words to songs, but they actually learn them phonetically by rote, without necessarily understanding them. This activity builds on the students' innate interest in popular music, while at the same time teaching them intensive listening skills.

Preparation:

1 Choose an English song that is currently popular in your country. Write the lyrics on a sheet of paper. If you don't know the lyrics yourself, there are many collections of lyrics available on the Internet.

2 Gap ten key words or phrases in the text. Make sure the gapped words are familiar to the students or can be understood through the song context.

Procedure

1 Hand each student a copy of the gapped text.

2 Play the song once through. The students may read along with their lyrics sheet, but they are not allowed to fill in the gaps yet.

3 Play the song a second time. This time the students can write words in the gaps. Give the students one or two minutes after the song has ended to finish filling in the gaps.

4 The students work in pairs and compare their results.

5 Play the song one more time and go over the song text with the entire class. Ask individual students to read each line.

Variation

For less advanced students, write the gapped words in mixed order at the bottom of the page for the students to refer to.

Follow-up

If your students are confident, you can close this activity with a *karaoke* competition. In this case, it is best to have at least three or four song texts available for the students to choose from. A less frightening alternative is to have the entire class sing the song once the gapped texts have been filled.

Comments

Be very careful when choosing song lyrics. Many popular songs have controversial lyrics which may not be appropriate for your students.

3.18 Music survey

Level Intermediate and above

Age 12–17

Time 90 minutes

Aims Asking questions and noting answers; analyzing, comparing, and evaluating data; working with numbers

Materials Photocopies of Worksheet 3.18 (one worksheet per student), calculators, poster paper (or access to computers in Follow-up 2); photocopies of each group's survey (one per student) in Follow-up 2

Surveys are an excellent way to generate interesting content for class discussion. They also provide you with valuable information about your students' ideas and preferences. Here we offer one or two examples of potential survey questions, but you can get even more language practice from the activity if you get the students to create the questions themselves.

Procedure

1   On the board write the following information. (You can substitute this information for any other data you might find more appropriate.)

- In 2003, 61.8% of US homes had at least one computer.
- In 2003, 54.7% of US homes had an Internet connection.
- In 2003, 92 % of students used computers at school.

(Source: US Census Bureau, 2003)

2   Ask the students if they are surprised by this information. Do they think the numbers would be the same in their country?

3   Explain that the information comes from a survey. Ask the students if they can explain what the word *survey* means. Tell them that surveys are made up of questions which give us information that we can turn into statistics.

4   Tell the students that you would like them to do a music survey. Hand out the music survey worksheet and ask the students to fill it in.

5   Split the class up into small groups of four to six students. Ask the students to combine their survey results into one total.

6   Ask each group to share the results with the rest of the class. Write the results for each group on the board and add them up to get a final total.

7   Tell the students that it is easier to look at the information in terms of percentages. Write a few examples of percentages on the board to highlight what you mean. Ask each group to work out the percentages for their individual results. While they are doing this, calculate the percentages for the final totals on the board. (Check that the students know the formula for calculating percentages.)

8 Bring the class together again and show them the total percentages. Invite the students to compare their group results with the results for the rest of the class.

Follow-up 1

Ask each group to write a paragraph summarizing the results of the survey. Have the groups compare their summaries. Did the groups interpret the data differently? Remind the students of the phrase *glass half full / half empty*. Interpretations vary depending on how you look at the data.

Follow-up 2

Have the class create a pie chart of the total survey results and smaller pie charts of the individual group results. Have the students glue the charts to a large sheet of poster paper. They can also do this activity on the computer as there are software programs that can generate pie graphs automatically.

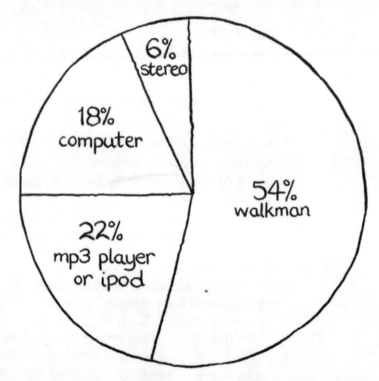

"How do you listen to music?"

Comments

For more activities related to music, see *Music and Song* in this series.

Worksheet 3.18

Music survey

Question	Answer
List your favorite types of music (rock, jazz, hip-hop, blues, punk, classical, rap).	
List in order of importance: music, TV, computers, sports.	
How long do you listen to music per day? (in hours)	
When do you listen to music?	
What do you use to listen to music? (CD player, Walkman, radio, MP3 player, cassette tape)	
What influences your musical taste? (parents, friends, radio, magazines)	
Should songs with violent or sexist lyrics be banned?	
What is more important, the sound of a song or the lyrics?	
Is it OK to download music from the Internet for free?	
Do you burn CDs on your computer?	

3.19 Surveys

Level	Intermediate and above
Age	12–17
Time	Lesson 1: 60 minutes; Lesson 2: 90 minutes
Aims	Asking questions and noting answers; analyzing, comparing, and evaluating data; working with numbers
Materials	Photocopies of each group's survey (one per student) for Lesson 2

Procedure

Lesson 1 1 Remind the students of the music survey you did in a previous class.

2 Explain that you now want them to create a survey of their own. They will need to write at least ten questions for their survey.

3 On the board write some potential survey topics, for example, *relationships, money, parents.* Elicit some ideas from the students as well.

4 Break the class up into small groups of four to six. Have each group select a topic for their survey and write at least ten questions.

5 Circulate and offer help where needed. Point out errors but try not to correct.

6 Once the students have completed their questions, have one student from each group type the final copy on the computer and print out a copy for you. If you don't have access to computers, ask the students to give you a clean legible handwritten copy. Make copies of the group surveys so that you have one copy of each survey for each student in the class.

Lesson 2 **1** Hand out the surveys to the students.

2 Give the students 30 minutes to fill out the surveys. Limit the number of surveys to three per person. If you have a very large group you may have to do this on two separate days.

3 Collect the surveys and hand them to the groups that wrote them.

4 Give each group 30 minutes to evaluate and quantify the information they received.

5 Ask students from each group to take five minutes to present their findings to the class.

Variation 1

Make the surveys oral. In this case, have students ask each other questions with the questioners noting the answers on the survey sheet. Move about the room and monitor for English language use.

Variation 2

Rather than conducting the surveys in class, if you work in a school, arrange with your co-teachers to have their classes take your students' surveys. If other classes in your school don't have an adequate level of English, have your students conduct the surveys in the native language and translate them into English when quantifying the data.

Variation 3

To simplify the surveys for quantifying, have the students create multiple-choice questions rather than open questions.

Follow-up

Conduct an Internet survey. Join a keypals group and find a partner school willing to participate in the survey. Maybe they will create a survey for you as well. You can make simple questionnaires for free using Zoomerang (www.zoomerang.com) and if you create a Yahoo group (www.groups.yahoo.com), there is also a polling function you can use for free.

3.20 Debates

Level Upper-intermediate and above

Age 14–17

Time 90 minutes (for the debate itself) plus time for practice and research

Aims Public speaking skills; active listening; note-taking; rhetorical phrases

Materials Photocopies of Worksheet 3.20; a timer

Debates are more than discussions. They are structured interchanges which require students to think and speak precisely. Debates require a good command of the English language to be effective in the language classroom, and are recommended for students at the higher-intermediate and advanced level. A debate can be about virtually any subject, but in the language-learning classroom we recommend sticking to topic areas where students have some background and previous knowledge.

Debate rules

First of all, every debate begins with a proposition—a statement—rather than a question. For example, instead of a question such as:
• Do you think music with violent lyrics should be banned?

a proposition would be:
• Music with violent lyrics should be banned.

As a first step in introducing the students to debates, you can prepare a series of questions and have the students turn them into propositions. As a follow-up to a survey activity (Activity 3.19), students can create propositions based on the results of the survey.

Once you have chosen a debate topic, you can decide to announce it a few classes before the debate and give students a chance to prepare in depth, or provide the topic at the time of the debate itself, giving students little time to prepare. We suggest giving the students the topic a few classes before the debate, but you could also give them an impromptu topic which is familiar enough for them to generate immediate and obvious arguments for and against.

In a debate, one team defends the proposition and the other team opposes it. It is important to make sure that the students understand that they must defend or oppose a statement regardless of their own views. A debate is not an exercise in personal opinion, but a public speaking competition.

In our EFL version of a debate we recommend that each team have four speakers. Each speaker has a specific role to play. Below is a table of speakers and recommended maximum speaking time. Remember that although the times may sound short, they are actually quite long, especially for a language learner. Try to speak for three minutes on a subject yourself sometime.

Teenager topics | 105

- First speaker: proposition arguments   3 minutes
- First speaker: opposition arguments   3 minutes
- Second speaker: proposition secondary arguments   3 minutes
- Second speaker: opposition secondary arguments   3 minutes
- Third speaker: opposition rebuttal   2 minutes

Worksheet 3.20

Debate judging

Proposition team	Made clear points	Spoke clearly and with few mistakes	Stayed in time limit / used time wisely	Total points
First speaker: proposition				
Second speaker: proposition				
Third speaker: opposition rebuttal				
Final speaker: proposition closing				

Team total points

Opposition team	Made clear points	Spoke clearly and with few mistakes	Stayed in time limit / used time wisely	Total points
First speaker: opposition				
Second speaker: opposition				
Third speaker: proposition rebuttal				
Final speaker: opposition closing				

Team total points

Photocopiable © Oxford University Press

- Third speaker: proposition rebuttal   2 minutes
- Final speaker: closing comments for proposition   2 minutes
- Final speaker: closing comments for opposition   2 minutes

Judging

When you are first introducing debates to your class, we recommend that you act as the only judge. If you can, you may want to invite other teachers at your school to join you on the panel. Later you can select a group of students to judge the events. This is an excellent activity for promoting active listening skills.

Each speaker is awarded points by the judges, which are recorded on the debate judging worksheet. After the debate, all the scores are collected and added together to find a winner. Each speaker is judged on a scale of 1–10 according to the following criteria.

- 10: a perfect speech (this should be a very rare score)
- 8–9: excellent speech
- 6–7: good speech
- 4–5: fair speech

You should only award a speaker a three or under if that speaker was unprepared or said something inappropriate, such as a personal comment about one of the other speakers.

Preparation

Before introducing debates it is a good idea to introduce or review key rhetorical phrases. These formulaic phrases will help the students structure their speeches.

Examples

- *In the first place …*
- *I agree / I disagree …*
- *On the other hand …*
- *On the contrary …*
- *For instance / For example …*
- *Nevertheless …*
- *However …*
- *In conclusion …*
- *To sum up …*

Procedure

1 Give each team 20 minutes to organize their speeches.

2 The first proposition speaker states the team's opinion and gives arguments to support this position.

3 The first opposition speaker introduces the counter arguments. Remember that the first opposition speaker does not answer the first proposition speaker, but sets forth his or her own arguments.

4 Give the teams five minutes to discuss and prepare arguments for the second speaker. The second speakers (for proposition and opposition) offer additional arguments to support their positions.

5 Give the teams five minutes to prepare their rebuttals. Explain to the students that in the rebuttal they must counter the opposing team's arguments.

6 The proposition team goes first in the rebuttal round, with a rebuttal of the opposition. The opposition team follows with the proposition rebuttal.

7 Give the teams ten minutes to prepare their final speeches. The final speeches should be a summary of their position, not an additional rebuttal. However, the closing speech can include arguments used to rebut the opposing team. The proposition team makes the first closing speech, followed by the opposition's final speaker.

3.21 Advice column

Level	Intermediate and above
Age	12–17
Time	60 minutes
Aims	Giving advice; conditionals; imperatives
Materials	English language newspapers or magazines with advice columns; photocopies of advice columns; index cards, scissors, and glue

Preparation

1 Before class collect newspapers or teen magazines with advice columns.

2 Photocopy the advice columns, questions and answers.

3 Cut out the questions and answers and glue them onto separate index cards or sheets of paper. Make sure you have one question or answer per student, or per pair of students.

Procedure:

1 Tell the class: *I have a friend and he has a problem. He wrote me a letter. Here is what it said.* Pretend to read: *Dear X, I'm a student at the local university. Everyday I eat lunch at the cafeteria and I see this beautiful girl. She looks at me too. The problem is that I am too afraid to talk to her. What should I do?*

2 Elicit some ideas from the students. See if the students use conditionals or imperatives. Write some phrases on the board:
- *If I were you, I'd …*
- *In my opinion, you should …*
- *It would be a good idea to …*
- *Whatever you do, don't …*

3 Hold up the index cards with advice column questions and answers. Mix the cards thoroughly and hand one card to each student (or pair of students). Give the students a couple of minutes to read their question or answer.

4 Ask each student to read their card. The other students listen and raise their hand if they have the corresponding question or answer and read it out loud to the class.

5 Divide the class up into small groups or pairs. Ask each group to write a short question for an advice column.

6 Collect the questions. Mix them up and redistribute them to the class. Now have each pair or group write an answer to the advice question they received.

7 Ask the students to read the questions and their answers. Ask the rest of the class if they agree with the advice. Invite them to suggest other ideas.

Variation

Make this a speaking activity. Make one half of the class 'advisors' and the other half 'questioners'. Have students move from advisor to advisor, asking the same question. Have them choose the answer they feel is best, write it down, and share it with the rest of the class.

Follow-up 1

Invite other classes to submit questions to your students (in English). In pairs or groups, have your students write down answers and return them to the other class.

Follow-up 2

Create a website where students can send email questions anonymously. Work with your class to provide answers.

3.22 Modern phobias

Level	Intermediate, upper-intermediate
Age	14–17
Time	Two 60-minute lessons
Aims	Vocabulary building; dictionary work; present and past tenses (for Follow-up)
Materials	A picture of a big furry spider or other animal that people may have a phobia about; photocopies of a gapped list of phobias and their definitions

Preparation

1 Write two columns on a piece of paper. Head the left-hand column *Fear of …* and the right-hand column *Phobia*. List fears and phobia names under these headings, including the following:

Examples
- fear of darkness   achluophobia
- fear of heights   acrophobia
- fear of open spaces   agoraphobia
- fear of cats   ailurophobia
- fear of pain   algophobia
- fear of vehicles   amaxophobia
- fear of men   androphobia
- fear of England   Anglophobia
- fear of spiders   arachnophobia
- fear of books   bibliophobia

2 Prepare a gapped version of this list by blanking out items at random from each column.

Procedure

Lesson 1 1 Hold up the picture of a spider (or other animal) and say, with exaggerated fear: *I'm afraid of spiders!*

2 Explain to the students that when someone is afraid of something to the point that the fear is irrational, we call this fear a *phobia*. Ask the students what they are afraid of and if they have any phobias.

3 Draw a line down the center of the board. On the top left side of the board write: *Fear of* …. On the top right side write: *Phobia*.

4 Ask the students if they can think of any common phobias. For example: *Fear of heights*. Write *Fear of heights* in the left column and *acrophobia* in the right. Continue with a few more examples:

Fear of flying – aerophobia

Fear of tight spaces – claustrophobia

5 Hand out the phobia list.

6 Tell the students that you want them to complete the list. Explain that each group can use a dictionary or the Internet. Give the students 30 minutes to complete the task or set it as homework.

Lesson 2 1 Go over the results of the phobia list with the students. Explain to the students that these are all classic phobias. Tell them that things are changing so fast in the world that we need new names for new phobias.

2 On the board write: *emailophobia*. Ask the students if they can guess what phobia this might be. Explain that it means fear of sending an email to the wrong person.

3 Split the class into small groups. Ask each group to come up with five new phobias that would impact modern teenagers.

4 Have each group present their results to the rest of the class. Did two groups share the same phobia but give it different names?

Follow-up 1

Ask the students if they can think of any phobias they used to have but don't have anymore.

Follow-up 2

Have students investigate whether any of the phobias they created really exist. What are they called?

Further Reading

Books

De Bono, Edward. 1978. *Teaching Thinking*. London: Penguin.

De Bono, Edward. 1977. *Lateral Thinking*. London: Penguin.

Ellis, Gail and Sinclair, Barbara. 1989. *Learning to Learn English*. Cambridge: Cambridge University Press.

Fisher, Robert. 1990. *Teaching Children to Think*. Cheltenham: Nelson Thornes.

Fisher, Robert. 1995. *Teaching Children to Learn*. Cheltenham: Nelson Thornes.

Gardner, Howard. 1985. *Frames of Mind: The Theory of Multiple Intelligences*. New York: Basic Books.

Gardner, Howard. 1993. *Multiple Intelligences: The Theory in Practice*. New York: Basic Books.

Grinder, Michael. 1995. *ENVoY: Your Personal Guide To Classroom Managemen:* Portland: Metamorphous.

Mosatche, Harriet. 2000. *Too Old for This, Too Young for That*. Minneapolis: Free Spirit.

Puchta Herbert and Schratz, Michael. 1993. *Teaching Teens*. London: Longman.

Salmon, Gilly. 2004. *Etivities*. Abingdon: RoutledgeFalmer.

Swados, Elizabeth. 2006. *At Play: Teaching Teenagers Theater*. New York: Faber & Faber.

Vygotsky, Lev M. 1986. *Thought and Language*, Cambridge, MA: MIT Press.

Websites

The Internet is filled with sites catering to teenagers, of which we can only offer a very selective few. Please be aware that internet addresses change frequently. If you find any links which are no longer working, check the companion website to this book on the Resource Books for Teachers website www.oup.com/elt/teacher/rbt for updates or to send us your feedback and suggestions.

Inclusion in these lists does not necessarily mean that the authors or publishers of this book endorse these sites or their content.

Teaching Languages to Teenagers

http://www.teachingenglish.org.uk
Lots of interesting ideas for teenagers. The methodology section has some good advice on classroom management and motivation.

http://www.teachingenglish.org.uk/
The British Council English teaching site

http://www.call4all.us
A huge collection on language learning links

General Teaching

http://www.educationworld.com/clsrm_mgmt/index.shtml
Huge website with lots of links to all aspects of education. US-based.

http://www.teachernet.gov.uk
Links to hundreds of useful sites. UK-based.

Debates

http://www.idebate.org/debatabase

Epitaphs

http://www.blakjak.demon.co.uk/epitfs.htm
http://www.epitaphs.us/
http://www.epitaphs.us/http://www.goblinville.com/epitaphs.htm
This one is especially good for the 12–14 age group.

History of Street Names

http://www.edinburgh.org.uk/STREETS/part1/a.htm
Edinburgh street names

http://en.wikipedia.org/wiki/Street_name
The wikipedia has a nice discussion of the etymology of street names with lots of international references. Please note that the wikipedia is a work in progress and constantly changing.

Idioms

http://www.idiomsite.com/
http://www.eslcafe.com/idioms/id-mngs.html
Provides examples in sentences.
http://www.idiomconnection.com/
Organizes idioms by topic area.

Music Lyrics

http://lyrics.com
http://www.musicsonglyrics.com
http://www.lyricsdomain.com

Names

http://www.behindthename.com

Phobias

http://www.phobialist.com/
This lists phobias in two ways—explanation first and phobia first.

Teen Issues

http://www.idealist.org/kt/index.html
Non-profit organization with links to projects and sites of interest to both children and teenagers dealing with issues such as poverty, the environment, and health.

http://www.thinkquest.org/library/cat_show.html?cat_id=206
A library of websites on issues of relevance to teenagers.

http://www.oup.com/elt/catalogue/teachersites/rbt/globalissues/weblinks/?cc=global
Web links from *Global Issues* in the Resource Books for Teachers series. Part of the Oxford Teachers' Club.

Teen Magazines (online and print)

http://www.seventeen.com/
Girl-oriented

http://www.bbc.co.uk/slink/index.shtml?/
The BBC teen site, with lots of links.

http://www.teenmag.com/

http://www.teenpeople.com/teenpeople/
Good for reading up on celebrities, with lots of pictures. This magazine is only available online.

http://www.teenink.com/
Written by teenagers

World Sports

http://en.wikipedia.org/wiki/List_of_sports
A constantly growing list of sports

http://sportsvl.com/
Links to a huge number of sports

http://obscuresportsquarterly.com
Very unusual sports

Stock Market

http://www.nyse.com/about/education/1098034584990.html
Educational materials produced by the New York Stock Exchange

Index

NOTE: References in **bold** type refer to Activities.